The Ways of the Wild

a practical guide to the outdoors

Kevin Callan

broadview press • 1993

Canadian Cataloguing in Publication Data

Callan, Kevin
The ways of the wild : a practical guide to
the outdoors
ISBN 1-55111-024-5
1. Camping. I. Title
GV191.7.C35 1993   796.54   C93-094691-X

Broadview Press
Post Office Box 1243, Peterborough, Ontario,
Canada. K9J 7H5

in the United Sates of America:
Post Office Box 670, Lewiston, New York
14092, USA

in the United Kingdom:
c/o Drake Marketing Services, Saint Fagan's
Road, Fairwater, Cardiff, UK, CF53AE.

Broadview Press gratefully acknowledges the
support of the Canada Council, the Ontario
Arts Council, and the Ontario Publishing
Centre.

Illustrations by Dave Fewster, except those on
pages 95, 137, and 139–43, which are by
Robert Tuckerman.

Printed in Canada

1 2 3 4 5 6 7 8 9 10 11

Contents

Chapter One:

BRINGING ALONG THE ESSENTIALS

Chapter Two:

BEFORE YOU GO

Chapter Three:

FOOD FOR THOUGHT

Chapter Four:

LOST AND FOUND

Chapter Five:

BEARS, BUGS, AND BEAVERS

Chapter Six:

SOGGY SURVIVAL

Chapter Seven:

BRUISES, BLISTERS, AND BAND-AIDS

Chapter Eight:

HOW TO BE A "GREEN" CAMPER

Chapter Nine

QUEST FOR FIRE

Chapter Ten:

COLD CAMPING

Chapter Eleven:

CANOE CAMPING

Chapter Twelve:

DARKNESS & SOLITUDE

Chaper Thirteen:

CAMP CRITTERS

Chapter Fourteen:

NAME THAT TREE

Chapter Fifteen:

READING THE STARS

Chapter Sixteen:

SNAP-SHOT MEMORIES

Chapter Seventeen:

A CAMPFIRE TALE

INTRODUCTION

If you sit and watch a group of campers the moment they identify their site and begin setting up camp for the night, you'll be amazed at the diversity of characters among them. There will be someone going off into the back forty in search of firewood, even though they packed a cooking stove and the air temperature is above 80°F (24°C). Others work in organized pairs setting up the tents or, being stricken with bear phobia, quickly throw a rope over a tree branch to later hoist the food pack. And last, but not least, a strong-voiced character stands in the midst of everything acting out the supervisory role.

In record time, however, the camp is set up and they all go off to do their own separate thing: the enthusiastic fisherman paddles out to the bay to wet a line, the supervisor catches a snooze in his cozy portable hammock, the camp chef begins to prepare a "surprise" for everyone, and the joker of the group spends his time looking over the chef's shoulder, constantly making smart remarks. His sarcasm is rewarded, however, when he is suddenly dubbed the "camp dishwasher" by the others.

Then darkness falls, the signal for the group to gather together around the glowing embers of the campfire and begin to reminisce.

I can almost picture myself sitting alongside my camping companions by the fire, looking back upon those endless portages we cursed along or remembering the times when rain gear became the fashion while we hiked along a soggy trail. In fact, I'm not sure about anyone else, but when my friends and I gather together to share stories around the fire about past trips, the bad memories usually outnumber the good. But without fail, after telling tales of our "misadventures," someone always ends up asking, "Well, where to next year?" Then, rushing with enthusiasm, we start planning a canoe route with longer portages or a hiking trip with a trail more rugged than the one before it.

During our last trip together I asked my friends one evening to tell me their reasoning behind spending their vacation time battling bugs and sweating over lengthy portages. The answer started off as a group smile, followed by an outburst of laughter, and then blank stares all around the campfire. Eventually we tried to share our true feelings. Mike said he appreciates the friendship reunions every year. Scott likes catching the biggest fish of the trip and then teasing everyone about it. I enjoy escaping the pressures of civilization to watch a sunset or listen to the wail of the loons. But not one of us could come up with a response good enough for everyone to agree upon, except maybe Doug. He simply stated, "The only way one could figure out why we do this every year is to go out and give it a try themselves." And then he jokingly added, "If only we could somehow make their trips a little easier by allowing them to learn from the mistakes we've made over the years."

In response, we all burst out laughing once again, threw another log on the fire, and then spent another hour telling "Remember when..." stories.

Come morning, while the camp chef was preparing breakfast and the avid fisherman was out trying his luck, the strong-voiced supervisor of our group made the decision that it was the job of the writer of the group, namely me, to follow Doug's advice. So "Trail Tips: A Camper's Guide For The Outdoors" was born. I hope you like it, and maybe even learn something from it — my life as a permanent camp dish-washer depends on it!

Chapter One:

Bringing Along the Essentials

CAMP STOVES

I teach a course called Environmental Issues at the local community college, so I guess it was fitting for the school to ask me to go along with the Parks and Recreation class on their annual canoe trip to teach the students how to practise low-impact camping. Treading lightly on the earth didn't go over so well with some "tradionalists," however, when I mentioned that only one campfire would be allowed during the five-day adventure, preferably on the last night of the trip. "How will we cook our meals?" they quickly asked. "With camp stoves," I replied. "Now you all have a week to go out and beg, borrow or steal a stove for the trip and I don't care what type it is."

A week later I found myself setting up camp for the first night with an angry mob, disappointed at having to crouch around an unfamiliar cooking stove rather than a cozy campfire. But as the days on the trail grew longer and the students grew wearier, not one of them felt the urge to gather wood and wait an hour before burning their meal over open flames. In fact, on the last night of the trip the group chose to sit out on the rocky shoreline and watch the stars rather than light up an evening fire.

Here are some of the camp stoves that were used on the trip, including comments on their advantages and disadvantages:

Optimus Hunter 8R ($100 and most expensive)

The student operating this stove had borrowed it from his older brother who threatened him with his life if he came back with it in pieces. There was no doubt, however, that even if the student hadn't continued to care for it throughout the trip the Optimus would have come back intact; it is one of the most reliable white gas fueled stoves available. Judging by the time it took him to get dinner on the go as well, it was obvious that the stove was easy to set up. There were some complaints about the rudimentary priming procedure, not to mention that the student kept on searing his fingers on the control key.

Trangia 25 ($60.00)

I think one of the salespersons down at the local outdoor shop took advantage of a few inexperienced student campers the moment they walked in the door looking for stoves: three of them had brand new Trangia 25s. I'm not saying it was a waste of money. The stove came equipped with a set of easy-to-clean nesting pots and a frying pan, and the students received bonus points for using a stove which burned alcohol instead of a petroleum product. The expensive contraption, however, had too short a burning time to cook an entire meal without refueling, and there was the added danger of having to adjust a flame one could hardly see by reaching into the stove and sliding a metal disc over the burner.

Camping Gaz Bluet 206 ($28.00 cheapest stove)

When the temperature dropped, the Camping Gaz Bluet 206 took longer to boil. This butane stove was least popular for cold camping, but for short summer outings the students figured it would be ideal. It is a clean-burning, reliable, and trouble-free stove operating on a pressurized canister that is attached to the stove and punctured to let loose the vaporized butane, which is then ready to set alight. The flame can be controlled easily and placed at a simmer, unlike many of the other stove models.

It was discovered later on the trip, however, that a half-full filled canister was not as efficient as a full one. A few students also made a good point when they questioned how "environmental" it was to throw all the used canisters in the landfill after our low-impact camping trip.

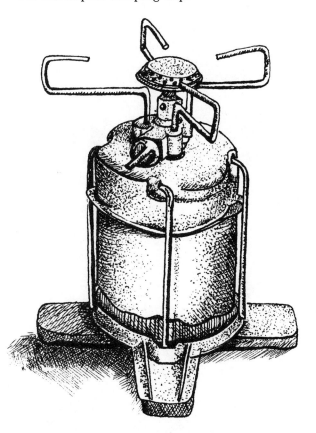

Coleman/Peak One ($55.00 best value for your money)

There's an assortment of Peak One stove models to choose from now: Feather 400, Multi-Fuel, and the new light-weight model with a separate attachable gas cylinder. One student on the trip packed along the Peak One Multi-Fuel because she had planned a trip to South America during her summer vacation and wanted to have a stove that could be run on either white gas or kerosene. The white gas was used during our trip. The Peak One seemed to do a great job getting the student's meal ready in a hurry, especially with the wind-screen she brought along for it. The stove, with its wide stance legs was very stable, but it was a tad heavy to carry and a real pain to nestle into a pot for storage.

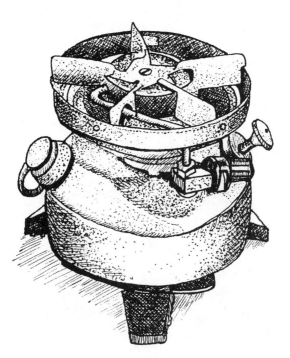

MSR Whisperlite ($75.00)

In our group I was the only one equipped with a white-gas burning MSR Whisperlite and I found myself constantly being criticized for the newly purchased MSR's seemingly dangerous flare-ups due to my lack of practise priming the stove. I also burned a few meals because I was unable to control the flame past the "on" or "off" stage. Burnt or not, however, my dinner was done in record time and the stove felt weightless in my pack during the day.

Since then, the stove has broken down more times than any other model I've owned. The advantage of the MSR is that, in most cases, it is easily taken apart and repaired in the field. When other stoves I've used have broken down, I've had to be pack them away and go back to depending on an evening fire for my hot meals.

STOVE TIPS

Reducing Flare-ups

Flare-ups occur when liquid gas exits the stove when the burner is cold. The large yellow flame forces everyone in camp to run for cover while the camp cook fiddles with the control to produce the safe, stunted blue flame.

Stoves which run on pressurized butane or propane canisters are not as prone to flare-ups as stoves fueled by white gas or kerosene. The bottled fuels immediately exit the jet as a vapor and not a liquid gas.

To avoid flare-ups on my MSR Whisperlite stove, I make doubly sure I have placed enough fuel in the priming cup and check it has almost burnt away to properly preheat the burner before I turn the switch to the "on" position.

Stoves which have no priming cup ignite by spraying a mixture of air and gas into the chamber below the burner, ready to be set alight. To have the mixture properly exit the stove you must pump up the stove enough to create pressure to form the spray. If the stove is not pumped as specified in the instructions, then liquid fuel leaks into the chamber, flooding and then flaring up until the extra fuel burns away. Once the flame calms down, the stove's pressure must be pumped back up before a second attempt is made.

Cold Starts

As stated above, butane stoves do not work as well as white gas or kerosene stoves when the temperature drops. If you do a lot of cold camping make sure to purchase the appropriate stove. I have found, however, that sticking a butane canister under the armpit or rubbing it between your palms can heat it up enough to get it going.

Strong winds rob more heat from a stove than cold temperatures. Therefore, a wind screen is a must. Even on warm, windless days, the screen will cook up your dinner more quickly and save valuable fuel.

Lighting Up Inside Your Tent

It's a good idea never to light your stove inside your tent. If the rain continues to fall and you forgot to bring along a tarp, there's not much else you can do if you want a hot meal, provided you do not have a white gas or kerosene stove prone to flaring. It's best to operate the stove inside the tent's vestibule with the flap rolled up to make sure there is proper ventilation. Never light the stove directly on the nylon floor and never remove butane or propane canisters inside the tent.

How Much Fuel Do I Bring Along?

The best way to judge your fuel consumption is to plan forty minutes of cooking time for dinner and twenty minutes for preparing a hot breakfast. Let's say you're going on a five-day trip. That adds up to four dinners (two hours and forty minutes of burning time) and four breakfasts (one hour and ten minutes). Now add an extra hour for a couple of hot soups for lunch or for unexpected cold weather robbing you of extra fuel. So, to be on the safe side, you can say that you need a little more than five hours of fuel for a five-day trip. My MSR stove burns very quickly and hot, with a pump/fuel bottle which holds twenty-two fluid ounces (3-4 litres) of white gas. That gives me plenty for the entire trip. If you have a butane stove which runs on pressurized canisters, then two canisters should be enough, with a little to spare.

SLEEPING BAGS

A sleepless night can mean a torturous day on the trail, so make sure the sleeping bag you purchase is ideal for the weather conditions you could find yourself in.

First you must decide what kind of camper you are: a mid-summer snoozer who's lucky enough to get a single, five-day holiday between late July and early August; an eager camper who heads out the first long weekend in May and then packs it in after the last weekend in September; or the hard-core winter camper.

The summer snoozer will be happy with practically any bag on the market, especially the ones on sale. The late-spring to early-fall camper should choose the versatile three-season bag, with a temperature rating of 15°F to 20°F (-12°C to -7°C. And the hard-core cold camper should be equipped with a body-hugging mummy bag with an even lower temperature rating. In addition, a vapor barrier should be added inside the bag to keep perspiration build-up to a minimum and a waterproof liner should be wrapped around the outside. This will improve the temperature rating by five or ten degrees. Unless you venture out in the snow more than three times a year or you are planning a three-month-long expedition to the Arctic, however, I would suggest you rent a winter bag for cold camping and purchase a good three-season bag.

Choosing the insulation inside the bag is probably the most difficult decision one must make. The two choices are down (the soft plumage of a goose or duck) or synthetic fibre. Down is lighter and warmer, but it's expensive (over $200) and loses its insulation abilities when it's wet; it also takes forever to dry. Hollofil, Quallofil, PolarGuard, and Polysoft (priced between $60 and $250) are the main synthetic insulating materials on the market. If these new-age bags happen to get wet they will still retain their loft and keep you warm. The synthetic bags, however, take up more room in the pack than a compact down bag.

The construction of the bag itself should also be a consideration. The rectangular shaped bag is more roomy than the constricting mummy bag, but it is not as compact (make sure to stuff a mummy bag into its sack instead of rolling it up before packing it away). The mummy bag also comes equipped with a lined hood to keep your body heat from escaping every time you roll over in the night. For greater warmth it is important to note how close the stitching is on the bag. The closer the stitching the better the insulation works. And for better ventilation during those uncomfortable warm nights make sure the sleeping bag's zipper extends around your feet.

Washing Up and Bag Storage

The cleaner the bag the warmer it will be, so it's a good idea to wash your sleeping bag before each excursion. It's villainous the way dry cleaners care for a bag: the insulation, both down and synthetic, is crushed by the powerful solvents used. Your washer at home is, most likely, a top-loading machine that dances across the floor when turned on, twisting your sleeping bag to pieces. The downtown laundromat's front-loading washing machine is your best bet, temperately tumble-washing your bag around and around when placed on the gentle cycle in cold water. Dry the bag in the drier, set on low, or shake well and hang to dry.

The bag should only be placed in its stuff sack while on the trail. If it is kept constantly compressed, it takes at least a couple of days before it reaches its maximum loftiness. When not in use make sure to hang the bag up on a hanger.

Sleeping Pads

The days are gone when, before going to bed, a camper layered the floor of the tent with a bed of conifer boughs — thank goodness. Now, for a cozy night's sleep, one must place a plastic or nylon groundsheet on the INSIDE of the tent, followed by either a foam sleeping pad or the more expensive, and more comfortable, Therm-A-Rest. The Therm-A-Rest, a self-inflating foam-filled air mattress, gives as much comfort as three foam pads together. If you don't suffer from back pain, however, you are just as well off with the much cheaper open or closed foam pad. To stop the sleeping pad from wandering around the tent floor through the night, place a cotton shell over it. The regular slippery nylon covers will slide out from under you.

BACKPACKS

External- Or Internal-frame Backpacks?

An external-frame backpack consists of a light-weight aluminum or aluminum alloy frame outside the nylon bag which holds your equipment. As the frame is external, the weight of your gear is held away from your body and is evenly distributed between your shoulders and hips. With the load being held up by the frame, however, the pack will tend to sway back and forth while you walk along the trail, lessening your freedom of movement.

The majority of backpackers are now switching to internal- frame packs which place the weight snug against your back. With the load hugging your body it's much easier to scramble up a hillside or cross-country ski across a frozen lake without losing your

balance. The disadvantage of short-term comfort, however, is long-term back pain.

Given the array of both external- and internal-frame backpacks, along with an added assortment of travel packs, rucksacks, and converted luggage bags, the only safe advice I can give to help pick an appropriate pack is to ask yourself: is the pack for short weekend jaunts or a month hiking across Europe? How much gear has to be stored on your back? And how much room is left on your credit card?

In the store, make sure to properly size the pack to your weight and build. If you purchase a cheaper, one-size-fits-all pack, make sure the adjustment straps have little give. A hip belt should conform to your hips, not your hips to the hip belt. Padded shoulder straps should have extra padding that provides comfortable cushioning and shape retention. Before you hike out with your new purchase, make sure to ask the salesperson to load the pack up with weights and walk around the store, just to make sure it fits nice and snug. Out on the trail is no place to discover you've made the wrong choice.

Waterproof Packs For Paddlers

In a futile attempt to keep my camping gear high and dry while canoeing I used to stuff my equipment into separate garbage bags before placing them in my internal-frame backpack. After a few days on the river, however, the bags became ripped and torn, spilling their contents everywhere.

Lately I've given up on this system and replaced my garbage bags and backpack with a waterproof Cascade Design Pro Pack. This specially-designed and moderately-priced bag for boaters was first developed by Dennis Hill of the Seatle Sports camping equipment company. Hill, while hospitalized for a knee injury, was inspired to combine the roll-down closure on an ice pack placed on his knee with the bottom design of a grocery bag.

The pack uses a suspension system reminiscent of internal-frame backpacks. It offers detachable padded shoulder straps and an anatomically shaped padded hip belt. The only thing it lacks is a padded back and vertical stays.

The first time I used the Pro Pack was on a river trip near James Bay. For four days it rained and hailed, but, when I stopped to make camp for the night after my hard day on the river, I was rewarded by a comfortable night's sleep in a dry sleeping bag.

Packing Your Pack

It only took a few hours of marching along the trail before a group of high-school students I was guiding on a hiking trip a couple of years ago started to complain about the heavy burdens strapped to their backs.

I called a break and then checked each student's backpack to see if I could suggest ways to lessen their load. After closely examining the variety of packs, ranging from high fashion to cheap hand-me-downs, I discovered it was not so much the contents they were carrying that was giving them bruised shoulders and lower back pain, but rather the way the gear was stored.

Two students, in particular, displayed the art of packing in a way I had yet to witness.

Scott, a tall and slender outdoorsman, managed to stuff his equipment into the upper portion of his pack in such a way that I was certain a bird flying by would mistake it for a sturdy perch.

Melissa, an undersized and inexperienced hiker, had somehow lashed her winter sleeping bag, thick mattress pad, an oversized parka and other loose paraphernalia to the bottom of her pack. The ruffled baggage protruded way out to either side.

With Scott always having to keep an eye out for low overhanging branches, and Melissa being unable to squeeze herself through closely knit underbrush, they looked like Laurel and Hardy walking alongside one another on the trail.

There's defintely a trick to loading all your camping equipment properly into one pack without looking like a comedian. First, it's important to separate the assortment of gear by placing various items (cooking set, food, toiletries, etc.) into individual nylon stuffsacks. Place each stuffsack into your pack in such a way that you never have to be constantly rearranging the contents every time you reach in to grab an item.

A well-organized backpack has the sleeping bag and clothes at the base. The cooking set, food, stove, and fuel bottle are placed in the middle, with the heavier items positioned closest to your back and shoulders. Make sure, however, not to have a hard-edged frying pan or plastic peanut butter container jabbing into your spine. Finally, the lighter items, plus the gear you might need in a jiffy (like your rainjacket or camera) should be on the top layer.

Most backpacks come with small side pouches. Use these for your odds and ends (map, compass, bug juice, water bottle, sunglasses, etc.) along with your first-aid kit, repair kit, and your "munchy" kit. A good pack is also equipped with straps and buckles to lash your tent and sleeping pad on top. Make sure you tie the tent so it will not sag and bounce up and down while you walk; anything hanging out from your pack immediately makes extra weight. Double check the knot used to dangle your favorite drinking mug onto the outside of your pack; if you're the last in line on the trail and the mug comes free, it will be lost forever.

Packing for a Day Trip

Whether you are lounging around the main campground or spending a week traveling through the interior by way of canoe or hiking trail, make sure to keep a day free for exploring. Some of my favorite times while at home in the woods have been spent clambering up hilltops to get a view of the country I'm traveling through, trekking through the bush behind camp looking for isolated moose ponds, or equipped with my rod and reel, searching out fish-infested lakes. These simple days away from the ordinary itinerary could end up being the "true" adventure of your trip.

The well-equipped daypack, weighing 10 to 12 pounds (4.5 to 5.5 kilos), contains enough gear to help battle bugs, blistering sun, sudden storms, and an unexpected night in the woods. Here are some of the essentials to pack away:

1. Rainjacket and pants
2. Extra sweater or fleece top
3. Spare socks
4. Sun screen and lip balm
5. Hat and sunglasses
6. Bug repellent
7. Map and compass
8. Swiss army knife
9. Nutritious lunch (plus a few high-energy snacks)
10. Light-weight camp stove and fuel
11. Butane lighter and waterproof matches
12. Water bottle and juice crystals
13. Compact first-aid kit
14. Flashlight
15. Light-weight nylon tarp and a ball of twine

Optional: journal, paperback book, fishing gear, camera equipment

Before setting off on your daytrip, secure your camp for the worst. I once laid out all my belongings to dry while I headed out to scale a nearby mountain. When I reached the summit, however, rain clouds suddenly appeared out of nowhere, blackening the sky, and flooding my camp down below with wind and rain. Also prepare for unwelcomed guests, such as bothersome bears who don't know the meaning of being nocturnal and unethical campers who rob you of some of your prize gear instead of purchasing it at the outdoor store like everyone else. Believe me, it happens!

TIPS ON TENTS

Before going out to purchase a tent keep in mind two very important points: the flimsy nylon dwelling you're about to buy will be your home away from home for the entire length of your trip. And, each time you pick up and go to another campsite, the tent has to go along with you.

The dilemma is that there is no roomy tent that is light to carry. So you must decide what is more important to you: space or weight.

I go on long trips, some lasting over a month, so I prefer to sweat a little when carrying my home on my back to ensure plenty of elbow room if I have to wait out a storm. But I'm more of an avid canoe-ist than I am a hiker, and to a canoeist a hiking trail is an endless portage. If I did spend more time hiking, however, I would opt for light weight rather than space without compromise.

Tents come in a variety of shapes, all of which have their merits. However, for affordability and ease of pitching up quickly before a storm hits, the free-standing dome or geodesic tent ($250 to $300) is my choice. This tent doesn't have to be staked down, so you can move it around quite easily once it's erect. This comes in handy in case it begins to pour in the middle of the night and you discover that your tent is pitched in the middle of a hollow. A vestibule attached to your front door is great. You can store lots of gear outside the tent, (especially those smelly sneakers) and cook up meals on your gas stove during a rainstorm. I would avoid making a habit of turning your vestibule into a kitchen while camping in bear country; a bruin might take a sniff of your tent, smothered in food smells, and mistake it for a snack.

Aluminum collapsible poles are much better than fiberglass. They may cost and weigh a little more, but the fiberglass eventually cracks and splinters, and replacement parts are expensive.

One final word of advice. The roof of the tent is made of a breathable nylon fabric but is not waterproof. That means the rainfly should cover the entire tent to keep you dry inside. Even the so-called "waterproof" sides can let water seep through the seams. Sealant from the hardware store should be applied every year for an almost guaranteed leak-proof tent.

MINI-TOOLBOX — DON'T LEAVE HOME WITHOUT IT

Long gone are the days when you patched the hole in the bow of the canoe with a piece of birchbark and heated pine gum or when you wove a backpack out of cattail shoots. If you happen to be equipped with a handy Swiss army knife, a roll of duck tape, and a few other small, quick-repair items, you're in business when that guaranteed unbreakable piece of camp equipment snaps in two. Here are a few essentials for your mini-toolbox.

THE COMPLETE REPAIR KIT

1. A small container filled with an assortment of screws, bolts, nails, and rivets to put back together split yokes, broken backpack straps, etc.

2. Epoxy glue for those "sticky" situations.

3. A strip of leather for repairing pack straps.

4. A roll of copper wire and/or strong string for lacing up canoe seats or even snaring a rabbit in a pinch.

5. Compact needle-nosed pliers for fixing anything and everything.

6. Needle and thread; those portable sewing kits are great.

7. Safety pins are almost as good as duct tape at times.

8. A spare flashlight bulb.

9. A Swiss army knife with all the extra gadgets one can afford.

10. Twist-tie — a great replacement for that tiny screw holding your eye glasses together, an eye missing from your fishing rod, or to clean out your gas stove.

11. Duct tape — lots of it!

12. It wouldn't hurt to pack away a little ingenuity as well, just in case you're forced to heat up the old pine gum!

THE ESSENTIAL HAT

There's nothing more essential on an outdoorperson's equipment list than their hat. Whether one's capped by a woollen toque, Aussie fedora, or the famous Tilley, a trip in the wilds is not complete without being crowned in character.

When I go fishing I trust the luck of my golf hat, complete with self-tied flies decorating its brim, more than I do my angling ability. Winter camping would be miserable without the company of my warm toque, with its bright colors and fluffy ball dangling on the top. And, last but not least, canoeing would be an impossibility without my durable baseball cap given to me by the owner of the Rugged Clothing Company.

BRINGING THE KIDS ALONG

Many outdoor enthusiasts simply give up camping when they have children. I know people who mourn the loss their of their former outdoor life-style and complain that, while they would love to get back out on the trail, their new responsibilities keep them out of the woods.

I also know people who claim that sharing a love of nature with children is a magical experience that adds a priceless component to their camping trips and their relationship with their kids.

Let's face it: kids require a lot of patience, especially on a camping trip. They slow you down and reduce the time you can spend in the interior so make sure the trips are always quality and not quantity. You may want to travel eighteen kilometeres a day, but your child probably doesn't. If you travel less than five kilometres but your child discovers a fluttering butterfly or watches an ant hill for an hour, that's great. A positive attitude packed along when camping with kids can mean the difference between a hellish trip to an unforgettable holiday. The secret is to adapt to the level of your children. Meet their needs on the trail, then yours. It is much easier for you to adjust to shorter, less strenuous trips than the child is to pushing all day without a break.

Start out on day trips or a long weekend at a provincial park to accustom both you and the child to camp life. Then slowly graduate to week long trips into the semi-wilderness. If you choose a canoe trip, paddle for only two hours to a main camp where there's a sandy beach for the kids to play at. It's also nice to camp with friends who have children around the same age.

One big disadvantage to travelling with the two-and-under crowd is packing along diapers. The cloth vs. disposable debate rages on. Both have their problems. Cloth diapers can be washed and dried at camp, but this means doing a serious laundry every day. Don't rinse them in the lake and be sure to dispose of diaper contents and rinse water in a treasure chest or cat hole.

Many parents find it easier to carry disposable diapers, carrying out the used ones in a garbage bag. I've seen people try to burn disposable diapers in the fire pit before leaving their site. The things don't burn but turn to big crusty globs of charred plastic goop making the campsite an eye sore for the next camper to come along.

One friend of mine recommends the stoop and scoop method. He packs disposables when camping with his one year old but lets the child go without diapers or pants for most days at the campsite.

Another idea is to pack along both cloth and disposable diapers, cleaning the cloth diapers on sunny days at camp and the using disposables for the rainy days on the trail.

Bill Day, a biologist at Lakehead University and father of fifteen-month-old Jonathan, is an expert outdoorsperson and a great camping dad. He strongly suggests spending a little extra money on camping equipment to ease your child's first adventure than it is to pay a babysitter every time you go for a paddle, hike, or ski. Bill used to hike with his son on his back until he purchased a baby jogger (a stroller with three large wheels and a slung seat). The baby jogger is designed for heavy off road use and is good for almost any terrain. He also bought a specialized sled to pull Jonathan along on his cross-country ski trips. Both pieces of equipment are expensive but for Bill and Jonathan it was money well spent.

Bill also recommends giving your child his or her own small day pack. Jonathan carries his teddy bear on portages and next year he will be able to pack along his own sleeping bag.

Bill admits that finding a PFD to fit his fifteen month old was a little tough. It's just like buying shoes for your child - a few months of wear and tear and you have to go out and buy another larger size.

Children dislike being cold, wet, and bug bitten just as much as you do. Make sure to dress your child as well as you dress yourself, using the layering technique. Large rain jackets with the arms rolled up or a poncho is suitable enough for rain gear. Be sure that you use a mosquito repellant that doesn't harm sensitive young skin (Johnson's Skintastic works well). Pack sneakers for use in the canoe and inside the tent and good old rubber boots for kicking around camp.

Pack along plenty of extra band-aids along with a collection of soothing words to help heal all the little cuts and bruises that are sure to appear.

Don't pack along a huge toy box: allow them to pack along only a few of their favorite toys. Once out there they will probably ignore even the few they brought and create their own from pine cones, sticks or weird shaped rocks. Have lots of games prepared for rainy days at camp or stories for the campfire at night. *Sharing Nature With Children* by Joseph Bharat Cornell is a great book filled with nature awareness games.

The last bit of advise is from Bill Day. At the end of our conversation he said something that made all the worry about camping with kids go away. "The biggest gift you can give to your child is to teach them to love what you love. If I have to carry Jonathan over a portage to do that than I will, because if I do it right he will end up carrying me over the same portage when he's my age."

BRINGING ALONG THOSE LITTLE EXTRAS

It is important to remember while preparing a camping trip that you are going on vacation and not heading out on an expedition. Keeping that in mind my canoe companions and I have always made room for a few extra items in our packs which may not be on anyone's regular equipment list, but that do add a little spice to each of our trips.

The annual tradition started a few years back while I was guiding a canoe trip in the north Kawarthas. The route was relatively easy, except for a long one-mile (1500 meter) portage. Halfway along the trail everyone began to complain about the distance I was forcing them to carry all their gear. The only way I stopped them lynching me was to tell them constantly that I had brought along a surprise which they could enjoy at the end of the day and which would make all the sweat and strain worthwhile.

By the time we arrived at our camp my partners couldn't wait for my surprise. They reached inside my pack and tore open the gift-wrapped package: a simple portable hammock tied up in a ball. They complained at first, since they had thought the surprise would be a bottle of brandy or a box of expensive cigars, but no one argued the moment they tried it out.

Since then we have taken turns packing along a gift: thermalounger, inflatable dish basin, pink flamingo lawn ornament, water wings, flask of Bailey's Irish Cream, cribbage board, candle lantern, and odor eaters, to name just a few.

We have also created an annual cooking competition for the first evening meal. Each canoe group pairs up to prepare a better recipe than the others. My regular canoe mate and I have mastered fresh fajitas, surf and turf, and shish kebobs.

So think twice before going super-lightweight; maybe that cozy hammock or fancy camp cuisine is well worth a little back pain on your next outdoor vacation.

Chapter Two:

Before You Go

A CONTACT PERSON MAY SAVE YOUR LIFE

Before driving onto the highway and heading out on your trip make sure to go over this list of items with your partner: Did you lock the door? Is the stove turned off? Have the plants been watered? Did the sitter pick up your pet budgy? Did you give your route and your approximate time of arrival to your parents?

Out of all those items on the list, the most important one is to make sure you have left detailed information about your trip with a check person. When you're completely lost in the woods or perhaps injured along the way, it is vital that someone back home knows your whereabouts so the search and rescue team knows where to look.

It is also crucial that you stick to the plan you laid out for the contact person, especially if traveling alone. I once forced myself to paddle 20 miles (32 kilometers) off-course while out on Georgian Bay so

I could use a telephone at a shoreline resort to call home and report I had decided to change my route. Two days later I slipped while portaging, twisting my ankle and bumping my head with the canoe. After a couple of Tylenol and constant soaking of the ankle in the cold waters of Georgian Bay, I was fine, but it made me feel a lot better knowing that I had called home beforehand.

It is also equally important to check in with your contact person the moment you arrive home. It would be a little embarrassing, not to mention expensive, if the police were conducting a search for you while you sat at home and watched their efforts on the six o'clock news.

HAVE YOU FORGOTTEN ANYTHING?

The following is a sample checklist for one camper for a five day trip during the warm summer months.

Clothes

- one cotton shirt
- two t-shirts
- one sweater or fleece top
- three pairs of underwear
- four pairs of socks (nylon/wool mix)
- two pairs of pants
- one pair of shorts (doubles as swim suit if you're not into   skinny dipping)
- boots
- sneakers, moccasins or sport sandels for around camp
- bug hat (finer mesh for blackfly season)
- bandanna
- hat
- raingear
- good sunglasses

Toiletries

- beach towel
- portable toothbrush and toothpaste (small tube usually found on sale at Drug store)
- toilet paper (one roll per person per week)
- hair brush
- biodegradable soap
- hair band
- razor
- contact lens solution
- glasses case
- birth control devices

Kitchen Set

- one medium and one small cooking pot with lids and non- stick frying pan (to avoid expensive cooking sets purchase all three seperately at department store and remove handles)
- plastic travel mug
- metal plate (plastic frisbee can be used as a plate, bowl and toy on the beach)
- hard plastic spoon and metal fork
- metal spatula
- aluminum foil
- camp stove with extra fuel container and funnel
- waterproof matches in waterproof container plus a butane lighter
- scouring pad and sponge mixture
- tea-towel
- pair of garden gloves for cooking on fire
- lightweight saw
- water bottle
- water purification gadget

- spices, jam, peanut butter, coffee, sugar, maple syrup, honey. margarine, etc... in various size, shape and style plastic containers.
- meals packed in seperate containers and in one large food bag.

Sleeping Gear

- tent
- ground tarp that fits inside the tent
- large rain tarp
- sleeping bag
- therm-a-rest or foam pad

Packs

- external or internal frame backpack
- stuff sacks for cloths and other items
- day-pack
- camera bag

Individual Items

- two 30 metre (90 foot) lengths of nylon rope
- flashlight with extra batteries and bulb
- whistle
- maps
- waterproof mapcase
- compass
- candles and candle lantern
- bug dope
- hand lotion
- camera, film, batteries
- playing cards, cribbage board, etc...
- fishing license
- camping permit
- first-aid kit

- repair kit
- extra zip-lock bags
- two or three garbage bags
- journel and pencil
- a good book paperback novel
- hammock
- bird, tree, animals track identification guide
- star chart
- fishing rod and small compact tackle box
- pocket knife

Canoeing Gear

- canoe
- paddle and one spare
- PFD
- bailer
- sponge
- knee pads
- portaging yoke and tumpline
- belt knife if river running
- tie-down strapes
- repair kit
- canoe cover if required

Chapter Three:

Food For Thought

Food has to be one of the most important items to pack for a camping trip. A combination of protein, vegetables, and starch have long been the key to refueling the body while venturing out in the wilds, especially when you are forced to go past your physical and mental limits to gain that extra distance before sundown.

Camp meals should be nourishing, lightweight, easy and quick to prepare, not to mention palatable. Dried foods sold in regular outdoor shops are ideal for campers, capturing a miniature lightweight and bacteria-free replica of home-style meals. But don't stop there. A number of other possible meals can be created by shopping at grocery or bulk-food stores.

THE SUPERMARKET TOUR

Before spending a fortune on store-bought freeze-dried foods, check out the local supermarket. You will be surprised at what you can pick up cheaply at the grocery store that is relatively lightweight and contains all the ingredients you need to conserve energy.

I frequently browse the aisles of my neighborhood supermarket and find an endless assortment of items to pack along on trips. Here are my latest discoveries:

Cereals

- Quaker Oats hot cereal packages (just add boiling water)
- Red River cereal
- Old Mill Minute Oats, Quick Oats, and Large Flake Oats cereal (ready in one minute)

Jam, Peanut Butter, Coffee, Tea, Cooking Oil

- Peanut butter and jam can be placed into a tube container at home

- Liquid honey (for tea and assorted dessert recipes)
- Tea (English Breakfast, Irish Breakfast, Earl Grey, and Cinnamon Stick are a few of my favorites)
- Coffee (instant, ground, or whole beans)
- Maxwell House Cappuccino instant beverage mix
- International coffees (Cafe Irish Cream, Suisse Mocha, French Vanilla, and Amaretto)
- Cooking oil (peanut or olive oil are great to bring along in small separate plastic containers kept in a ziplock bag in case they leak)

Instant Potatoes, Salt-free Spice, Juice Crystals

- Soft roll dumplings
- Potatoes Au Gratin with cheddar cheese sauce
- Lipton Potatoes and Sauce (Romanoff, Sour Cream and Chives, Scalloped)
- Idahoan Au Gratin Potatoes In Mix (Scalloped, Spicy Cheddar Potato Mix, Creamy Ranch)
- Diet foods should never be brought on any camping trip but Mrs. Dash, a salt-free spice, can be found in the diet section of the supermarket and is a great additive for many recipes.
- Juice crystals (Tang, peach, and orange flavor that come in packs of three or the sixteen ounce (480 gram) packs which can be poured into a used plastic peanut butter container are my picks)

Beef Stew In A Bag, Canned Tuna, Dried Soups

- Magic Pantry needs no refrigeration, is ready to eat after being placed in boiling water for two minutes and has tasty beef stew, cabbage rolls, lasagna, and chili, to name just a few. The containers are a little heavy, however.

- Canned tuna, chicken, salmon, sardines, baby clams, escargots, pate with perigord, smoked mussels, or oysters can make a bland meal into camp cuisine. But cans are heavy, and are illegal in many provincial parks.

- Dried soups (Sapporo Ichiban and Maruchan Raman Noodles make up a good hot lunch, along with Knorr's various dried soup mixes and Lipton's Batman Soup featuring the Penguin).

Spices, Desserts, Baking Needs, Storage Bags

- Seasoning mix (Knorr, French's, or McCormick's Spaghetti Sauce, Herb and Garlic, and Romaglio are lightweight and excellent to spice up regular noodles)
- Jello Pudding and Mott's Fruit Cups
- Muffin and loaf mixes are great to have, especially if you have a reflector oven.
- Pancake mix and syrup with blueberries, freshly picked at camp
- Tea-Bisk or Bisquick for easy-to-make pancakes, tea biscuits, or cinnamon rolls
- Ziplock bags for storing each meal separately
- Aluminum foil to bake fish or even potatoes, if you are crazy enough to carry them with you

More Marvellous Munchies

- Quaker Chewy Fruit Dipps and Granola Bars
- Pop-Tarts
- Betty Crocker Fruit Roll-ups

Pita Bread, Bagels, Candy, and Popcorn

- Pita bread (with preservatives)
- Bagels
- Candy (jelly beans, ju jubes, gum drops, smarties, M&M's, chocolate kisses, and a couple of Snickers bars)
- Popcorn kernels (no camping trip is fully equipped without them)

Rice, Pasta, The Famous Macaroni and Cheese

- Rice dishes (Lipton's Rice and Sauce, Uncle Ben's Exquisine's Rice and Noodles, Zesty Tomato Rice, Pilaf With Kidney Beans are great with pita bread)
- Pasta Noodles and Sauce (Lipton's Pasta and Sauce, Uncle Ben's Exquisine)

BULK FOOD BONANZA

The most difficult part of planning my first extensive solo canoe trip, was figuring out what to eat.

The food I brought along had to be extremely light, packaged in single servings, and, above all, inexpensive. Store bought freeze-dried foods, which I had used on many other trips with my regular camp friends, were out of the question this time. They didn't weigh much, but the packages were made for two people and I would have to take a loan from the bank to purchase enough for thirty days.

It was by pure luck that I walked past a bulk food store one afternoon and found the answer to my problem. With a little help from the store owner, who happened to be an avid camper, and a fifty dollar bill, I left with dozens of cheap nutritious recipes made up of seven simple cooking staples: lentils, rice, pasta, soy grits, couscous, bulgur, and quinoa.

Lentils

The common Egyptian lentil can be found in most bulk food stores. Cooking time can be reduced if you use the decorated lentils which are split and have their outer husk removed.

Rice

There is an endless assortment of rice that can be used in many different recipes. A teacher who works with me at the local college once told me how he lived off rice and wild greens while paddling in northern Quebec for an entire summer. He's not someone I would choose to be camp cook during a regular camping trip, but I bet his food pack was as light as a feather.

Mixing rice with lentils makes an excellent dinner after a long strenuous day on the trail. Eaten together they provide a richer balance of protein then when separate.

Pasta

Pastas can be bought at any supermarket, but whole-grain and vegetable pasta, more colorful and better for you, can be found at the bulk food store. Add a little dried tomato powder and a dash of spices, and you've got a meal fit for a king.

Soy Grits, Bulgur, and Couscous

For a quick, high protein dinner, try soy grits (cracked soybeans) or the more filling grain-like pasta called couscous.

Bulgur, cracked wheat that has been parboiled and dried, is also a quick staple for nutritious meals.

Quinoa

My favorite cooking staple, however, is a recently discovered grain from Peru. This "mother grain" is found in Andean Mountain regions of South America and is called Quinoa (pronounced keenowa). It contains more protein than any other grain and is even a complete protein by itself. It is also high in fiber, minerals, and vitamins — making it an ancient food staple for the Inca civilization, as well as the present-day hungry camper.

Quinoa can replace any grain in any recipe; just remember to shorten the cooking time to fifteen minutes or until all the water is absorbed. The grains will turn from white to transparent when done.

Of course, none of these simple cooking staples mean a thing without following recipes from the professionals (Simple Foods For The Pack by the Sierra Club, *The Nols Cookery* and *Wanapitei's Cookbook* are great guides). Or you can have fun by transforming your kitchen at home into a make-shift science lab for a few weeks before your trip, inventing your own recipes. The ultimate test of choosing the best recipes for your trip, of course, is to invite your friends over for dinner and feed them such dishes as Mushroom Bulgur Bonanza, Mountain Gruel, or Moroccan Couscous, making them believe you have spent all day in the kitchen cooking up these gourmet delights instead of twenty minutes over your camp stove on the back porch. If your guests enjoy the meal, pack the recipe in a ziplock bag for your trip, and, if they feed it to the dog, then I suggest you go back to the old drawing board.

TRUE GRIT:
HOW TO MAKE REAL CAMP COFFEE

Apart from the assortment of necessities stuffed away in my backpack, there's one small item that can either make or break any camping trip — camp coffee.

On many canoeing ventures the thought of a fresh-brewed cup of coffee over an open fire was the only thing that kept me going on the last portage of the day. And during winter excursions coffee was not merely a survival tool: it became the only thing that could drag me from the warmth of my sleeping bag on those bitter cold mornings.

If you are a true camp connoisseur then you'll agree that instant, perked, or filtered coffee has no place among the glowing embers of any breakfast fire. True camp coffee is nothing but real grounds-and-water-in-the-pot coffee. The ingredients of "true grit" are simple — one generous tablespoon of coffee per cup of water.

If you want to get carried away with tradition, the original outdoor coffee is created from the essentials. To start off you toss green coffee beans into the frying pan over an open fire, making sure to stir them now and then to keep them from sticking. Once the beans have turned brown and have excreted their famous aromatic fumes, you wrap them in a piece of cloth (your bandanna is a good stand-by), pound them with a rock until they're ground into little bits and pieces, and then immediately throw them into the pot to be brewed up.

Roasted whole beans can be bought if you don't have access to green beans. And if the rock pounding seems a little barbaric, grind the beans before your trip or pack along preground coffee, keeping it in an airtight container.

The ingredients of camp coffee, however, are not as important as the way in which they are added to the pot.

The technique which, I think, leads to the best results is to measure the right amount of water in the pot, then bring the water to a rolling boil, take it off the heat source, stir in coffee grounds, and let it steep (covered) alongside the campfire for approximately ten minutes.

Some people prefer to settle the grounds by throwing in pieces of egg shell or tossing in a few round pebbles. I've even witnessed campers take hold of the wire handle on the pot, swing it with the speed of an aircraft propeller, and have complete faith in centrifugal force. This suicidal action will pull the grounds to the bottom of the pot — guaranteed. I merely tap the side of the pot and make sure I let someone else help themselves to the first and last cup, so my brew is mostly free of any tiny granules.

The most crucial element of brewing "true grit" is never to let the coffee boil. Old-timers used to say that boiled coffee tastes like rotten shoe leather, and they're right!

The reason for the bad taste of boiled coffee is in the bitter tanic acid and flavoring oils it contains. The tasty oils are released at 205°F (86°C), just below boiling point. The bitter acids, however, are released right at or just above boiling point.

Any way you brew it, camp coffee should be enjoyed fresh from the pot to guarantee that extra push you need along that long portage or early-morning cold front.

WILD NUTRITION

Many of Canada's first settlers who sailed over from Europe died during their first winter from vitamin C deficiency, not knowing that a simple cup of pine needle tea, brewed from the trees growing all around them, could have saved their lives.

Today, people tramping through the woods can pack a cache of Earl Grey to obtain necessary nutrients, but it's always nice to know that one can resort to steeping a few pine needles or other types of foliage to prepare a somewhat adequate, if not more flavorful cup of tea.

Pine needle tea, with a teaspoon of sugar, has always been my favorite, hot or cold. Many other conifers can be brewed, however. Red pine is not as sweet as white, as it has a smoky aroma. White and black spruce make too hardy a taste for my liking, but cedar brews up nicely.

Among the species of deciduous trees, twigs from yellow birch saplings have to be one of the most delicious, giving off a light wintergreen aroma and taste. White birch can be brewed, making a dark red tea which lacks the wintergreen taste. The problem with gathering birch twigs is identifying. Young saplings do not have the familiar yellow or white papery bark, but rather have a reddish bark similar to wild cherry, which both smells and tastes extremely bitter.

Certain plants growing along the forest floor also make fine wild brews. The wintergreen plant, common to the boreal forest of Ontario, with its cluster of white and/or red berries (which taste a little like bruised apples) and small shiny leaves, has a stronger wintergreen taste than the yellow birch; maybe too strong.

Wild strawberry produces a mild, refreshing tea, and, like all the previously mentioned trees and plants, is rich in vitamin C.

To prepare these beverages at tea time, simply grab a handful or two of needles, twigs, or leaves and let them steep in boiling water for five to seven minutes.

Remember to conserve these natural nutrients by collecting only as much as you need, leaving the rest to ensure a continuous harvest. Unlike in the past, tasting teas from the wilds is not usually an act of survival, but rather a way to spice up your stay in the outdoors.

SEVEN SUCCESSFUL RECIPES

Chef Robert's Fresh Fajitas (serves two)

This recipe won my canoe partner, Scott Roberts, first prize during the annual cook-off competition my camp friends and I have for the first night on the trail.

1 sirloin steak

marinade sauce:

1/4 cup olive oil
1/2 cup red wine vinegar
1/4 cup barbecue sauce
1 cup (250 gram) block of cheddar cheese (grated)
1 cup mild salsa
6 oz (175 gram) container o fplain yogurt
1/4 head of lettuce
1/4 to 1/2 cup of water
6 tortilla shells
4 oz (100 ml) plastic container of olive oil

Cut steak into small strips and soak in marinade sauce overnight. Then place in a ziplock bag and store it in the freezer until just before your trip. Also freeze the salsa sauce in a leakproof container.

Coat the bottom of a frying pan with olive oil and fry up the strips of steak. While the steak is cooking, heat up the mild salsa. Once the meat is cooked, place it by the fire to keep warm while you prepare the rest of the recipe.

Coat the frying pan with olive oil once again and put in a tortilla shell, rotating it so it is evenly coated. Let the shell sit for ten seconds and then flip it over. Now put three strips of steak to the middle of the tortilla, two tablespoons of the salsa and some grated cheese. Pour a drop or two of water into the frying pan and cover for fifteen to twenty seconds or until the cheese has melted. Then slide the tortilla shell out of the frying pan and onto a plate. Add a tablespoon of plain yogurt and some lettuce. Fold the bottom and top of the tortilla in and both sides over. Enjoy!

Oodles Of Noodles (serves two)

1 sweet red pepper, sliced
1 cup of mushrooms, sliced
1/4 cup crushed walnuts
1 garlic clove
pinch of oregano
pinch of dried parsely
1 cup Parmesan cheese
1 1/2 cups small shelled noodles
4 cups water

While the noodles are boiling in a pot of water, fry up the garlic until it's slightly brown, and then add the sliced mushrooms and sweet red peppers along with the parsley and oregano.

Drain the noodles after fifteen minutes, add the peppers and mushrooms, and sprinkle on the Parmesan cheese and walnuts.

Mock Shepherd's Pie (serves two)

I have yet to win our annual cooking competition. It's not that my meals taste bad, but because I only use dried lightweight ingredients. I can't help myself. It seems every year I desperately try to make my pack weigh a little less than the year before. However, after my friends tasted my Mock Shepherd's Pie, they did give it an honorable mention.

2-4 cups water
1 cup bread crumbs
1 cup precooked rice
1 cup mixed dehydrated vegetables
(carrot, onion, green pepper)
1/4 cup dehydrated mushrooms
1 tbsp. parsley flakes
dash of garlic powder
1/2 cup bulgur
1 cup potato flakes
1 beef bouillon cube
dash of Worcestershire sauce
1 tbsp. tomato or spaghetti sauce powder

Combine the precooked rice, vegetables, mushrooms, parsley, garlic powder, beef bouillon cube, and tomato powder into two cups boiling water and let simmer for five minutes. Remove from heat and add bread crumbs. Stir until all crumbs are evenly moistened. Let stand for five minutes.

Place bulgur into two cups boiling water and let simmer for five minutes. Then add a dash of Worcestershire sauce and combine with the rice and bread crumb mixture.

Slowly add water to potato flakes until fluffy and place on top of the rice, bread crumb, and bulgur mixture. Add a pinch of pepper or Mrs. Dash salt-free spice before serving.

Al's Couscous (serves two)

Al MacPherson, a workmate and fishing buddy, is like any true avid angler: he's blessed with the gift of the gab. I'll always remember the time we were sharing a cup of coffee, exchanging tales of past fishing trips, when he accidently slipped out the whereabouts of his "secret" fishing spot in Algonquin Provincial Park. To keep me quiet he has paid a high price — his delicious couscous recipe.

4 cups water
2 cups couscous
1 tbsp. chicken soup base or choice of 1 bouillon cube
(beef, vegetable, chicken)
3 tbsp. of dehydrated mixed vegetables
1 cup grated cheddar cheese
3 tbsp. margarine

Bring water, chicken or other base, and dried vegetables to a rolling boil. Add couscous and margarine and stir well. Cover and cook on low for five to ten minutes. Check frequently as it can burn easily.

Once couscous grain is dry and light, remove from heat. Stir in cheese and cover until the cheese has melted. Season with Spike (all-purpose seasoning).

Bon Echo Bon Appetit

I don't always spend my time trudging through the wild interior. Many weekend trips are enjoyed car camping at a variety of provincial or national parks. Bon Echo Pronvincial Park is a favorite of my wife, Alana, and mine. But one July weekend, the constant rain and cold temperatures made it seem like the last weekend in October: we spent the entire two days huddled under a rain tarp playing endless hands of crazy eights, re-reading our favorite novels, and cooking up some of the best meals we have ever tasted. The following soup was the cream of the crop.

4 cups water
1 package chicken noodle stock or base
2 pieces of fresh chicken breasts
1 cup mushrooms
5 to 7 asparagus stalks

Grill chicken over open fire, cut into strips and mix together with the chicken noodle soup stock and mushrooms in boiling water. Let simmer. Add asparagus fifteen minutes before serving. The great thing about this recipe is that by letting the soup simmer all day, you can add extra ingredients for guests that wander by your campsite asking what smells so good.

DELIGHTFUL DESSERTS (serves two to four)

My camping companions and I do not compete with desserts, basically because I always cook them and they always taste great! Here are two of my favorites.

Simple Cinnamon Rolls

1 to 1 1/2 cups of water
3 cups Tea Bisk or Bisquick mix
1/2 cup brown sugar
1 tbsp. cinnamon
1/4 cup raisins
3 tbsp. margarine
flour for rolling

Mix Tea Bisk or Bisquick mix with water and roll out on floured canoe paddle. Spread margarine onto flattened surface, sprinkling on cinnamon, brown sugar, and raisins. Roll up into a log and slice 1 inch (2.54 cm) slices and place them in frying pan. Cover and bake over hot campfire coals.

Basic Biscuits (6)

1/4 cup water
1 cup Tea Bisk or Bisquick mix
handful of raisins or fresh-picked blueberries
flour for forming

Mix Tea-Bisk or Bisquick with water and stir in raisins or, if season and habitat permit, fresh blueberries. Spoon out medium-sized portions onto lightly floured surface and knead gently four to five times. Place in ungreased frying pan, leaning pan against campfire stones at an angle to a bed of hot coals to bake to a golden brown. Don't rush them or the bottoms will burn. Add a glob of jam to each and serve.

Chapter Four:

Lost and Found

To most people the thought of heading off the beaten path is terrifying. We have become so dependent on trails to lead the way — from hikes in the woods to portaging between lakes — that the idea of "bushwacking" is simply unthinkable!

To become completely comfortable with traveling in the outdoors one must, however, put aside one's inhibitions and break free from the trail — with a map and compass in hand, of course. I'll never forget the time I was leading a group of high-school students through the interior of Ontario's Killarney Provincial Park. We were more than halfway along the rugged Silhouette hiking trail, only to be stopped by a build-up of spring snow and slush.

The other leaders and I decided it would be best to travel cross-country, keeping along the southern slope where most of the snow had already melted.

So I took two steps off the marked trail and asked Chris to take a compass bearing off his map and lead the way.

Chris, who had aced map and compass skills on his mid-term exam, suddenly panicked, yelling out, "I can't do that. I'll get us all lost!"

"Now, Chris," I asked, "how can you get us lost if you have both a compass and a map to help you out?"

Chris then pulled out his map and compass, spun the map and shook the compass, and said, "I can't make nothing of all this. There's nothing to follow."

After watching Chris fumble around for ten minutes, I soon realized it was time to work for my keep and teach him the ropes. "Chris, don't panic. Marco Polo got lost halfway around the world and was eventually able to guide himself back home. You can at least find your way down this valley to the west so we can make camp for the night. Just remember what we did in class and you'll get us there in no time," I explained.

Chris scratched his head, thinking back to the lessons I had given him back at school. He began to regain his confidence. After some quick calculations, he ordered us to follow him into the unknown. A few hours later we made camp alongside an isolated lake set in the midst of the forested valley and Chris received an A+ on his practical exam by following a few simple steps and some good old common sense.

CHOOSING BETWEEN A MAP OR COMPASS

It's obvious that while navigating through the wilds it is best to be equipped with a map and a compass. But what if you had to make the choice between the two? What if the bushplane you were flying in crashed in the middle of nowhere? You have only seconds to leave the burning plane before it explodes and you only have time to grab either a detailed topographic map or a compass. Which one would you choose? I'm constantly surprised how many people choose the compass. Sure, with a compass you can discover which way is north, but where does that leave you? What if, unknown to you without the aid of a map, a wilderness resort is only a mile (two kilometers) south. You decide to travel north, however, not knowing that endless bush lies ahead. You can find north without the aid of a compass (covered later in the chapter), but there are no Boy Scout tricks to replace a good topographic map.

MAP SKILLS

I have paddled for up to three months, carrying both a map and a compass, and, even though I am glad to have a compass handy, I rarely take it out of my pack. Topographic maps place the lay of the land right in your lap. Paddling with a detailed back-country blueprint is like driving cross-country with a detailed roadmap. You can travel from point A to point B along the highway by looking out for road-side cafes and small hamlets. Traveling in the back-country you can do the same by spotting river mouths, islands, and rock outcrops.

A good topo map can be judged on its scale (the smaller the scale the less detail can be shown), age, the size of area it covers, types of symbols shown (it is good to know if a swamp blocks the trail or a falls is ahead on the river), and its contour interval.

The wavy brown lines on the map are the contour lines. They mark where the position of land is above sea level. Every fifth contour line, called an index contour, has the elevation marked somewhere along its length. If the lines are far apart then the land-scape is relatively flat. If the lines are close together then you can be sure the grade is quite steep. To figure out which way a creek or river is flowing, simply take a look at the contours. The closed ends of the contour line point upstream.

After you have taught yourself how to read your map, it's time to prepare it for your trip. First you must make the map waterproof. In the past I have tried large ziplock plastic bags or cheap map holders with built-in zippers; it didn't take long to trash either of them. If you happen to have use of a lami-nator, that's great. Laminating not only completely waterproofs the map, but you can even write on it. Some people prefer "Thompson's Water Seal," avail-able in both aerosol can or tins from your neigh-borhood hardware store, this only makes the maps water-repellent. Personally, I like my "Granite Gear" map case (made in the U.S.A.). It is equipped with a velcro flap and shock cords on each side for easy attachment to either your pack or the canoe thwart.

It's a good idea to trim away the sections you do not need. I once purchased the entire map collection for the Missinaibi River, starting from the town of Missinaibi all the way to Moosonee (265 miles/426 kilometers). There was no way I could pack all eighteen maps in their entirety, so I snipped off everything except the river itself, leaving me with a small bundle of detailed topos.

In Canada you can order updated topographic maps from:

> Canada Map Office,
> 615 Booth Street,
> Ottawa, Ontario.
> K1A 0E9
> Tel. (613) 952-7000 Fax. (613) 957-8861

- It may be best first to order the updated Index Map. Once you have located the area you wish to travel, then order by grid number, e.g., Map Number 31 G/5.

- The Canada Map Office recommends the purchase of your map requirements from the authorized topographical map dealer in your area. Many dealers advertize in the Yellow Pages under MAPS. Lists of authorized map dealers for each province may be obtained from the Canada Map Office.

COMPASS SKILLS

The best compass for any outdoorsperson is an orienteering compass. When I graduated from college
in 1984 and began working as a forest technician in
northern Ontario, the first item I purchased was a
Silvia orienteering compass. It was complete with
the standard features: a magnetic-tipped needle, a
compass housing marked with an orienting arrow
and orienting lines, a graduated dial, a base plate
which doubles as a ruler (measuring in inches and
centimeters), and an index line. My compass also
had a few extras, like a pre-set declination screw and
a mirror with a "bulls-eye" attached on top. The
mirror is for reading a bearing while holding the
compass at eye level, but I mostly used it to check
my hair in the morning.

What's great about the orienteering model is that
it has a built-in protractor, allowing you to calculate
direction and scale distance without orienting the
map to north.

The red end of the floating arrow always points
to "magnetic" north, not "true" north. "Magnetic"
north is farther south than the "true" or "geographi-
cal" north pole. The difference in degrees between
these two norths is called "declination." The declination varies depending on where you are in the
world.

If you are already confused, it's best to purchase
an orienteering compass complete with a declination screw. By turning the screw to the left or right
(east or west), you can pre-set the designated declination and never have to worry about it again. If
your compass doesn't come with a declination screw
than you must calculate the change in your bearing
each time. To do this, simply memorize the following formula: East is least and west is best. For example: If the declination is seven degrees east then
subtract seven degrees from your magnetic bearing.
If the declination is seven degrees west then add
seven degrees to your bearing. For example: 219

(magnetic) - 7 (declination) = 212 (true); 8 (magnetic) + 7 (declination) = 15 (true)

It is important to note that the north arrow on topographic maps points to true north.

To find out the declination for your travel area, contact the local district office of the Ministry of Natural Resources, National Park Service, or surveying company working in that region. Your topographic map should, however, have the declination value marked on a diagram in the lower map margin.

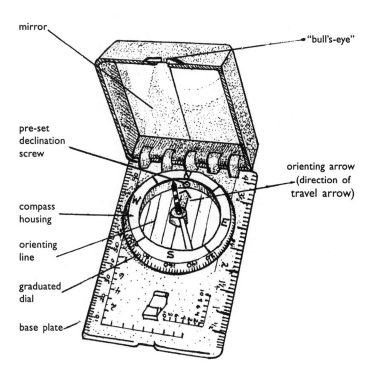

mirror

"bull's-eye"

pre-set
declination
screw

orienting arrow
(direction of
travel arrow)

compass
housing

orienting
line

graduated
dial

base plate

Taking A Field Bearing

A field bearing is a bearing calculated without the help of a topographic map. Say you are canoeing along a lake and you decide to stretch your legs a little and go off ridge-hiking. After paddling into a calm bay and beaching your canoe on shore, you head for a high ridge by walking through a stand of tall white pine. An hour later and you find yourself on top of an exposed ridge, trying to decide how you are going to find your way back through the pines, and come out exactly where you beached your canoe which you can spot on the shore below. To locate the direction you want to travel through the thick forest below simply do the following:

1) Place your feet firmly together and hold your compass level, at chest height.

2) Point the direction-of-travel arrow at the beached canoe (B).

3) Rotate the compass housing until the orienting arrow is perfectly in line with the red pointed end of the compass needle.

4) Read off the bearing lined up with the direction-of-travel arrow.

5) Follow the bearing (set in degrees) and you will walk out right to your canoe.

6) If you are halfway through the stand of pines and wish to make sure you're headed in the right direction, take a back bearing. Rotate your body around, holding the compass level, until the white end of the compass needle is lined up with the north end of the orienting arrow. If the ridge you just hiked from is in line with your direction-of-travel arrow, you've got nothing to worry about.

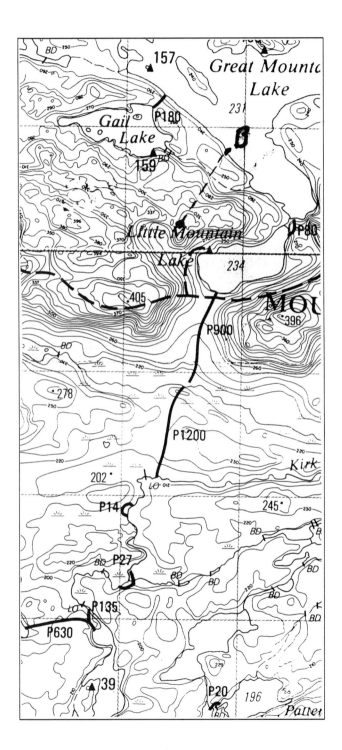

MAP AND COMPASS SKILLS

To figure out how to utilize a map and compass, let's look at the steps that Chris, my high-school student, followed while leading us through Killarney's interior. (See diagram)

1) Chris first marked the letter "A" on the topographic map at the point where we walked off the trail. Then he marked the letter "B" at a designated campsite on Sandy Lake (marked by a red triangle).

2) By using the baseplate on the compass as a ruler, Chris drew a line in pencil from A to B, pointing the direction-of-travel arrow towards the letter B.

3) Without moving the compass itself, Chris then rotated the compass housing until the orienting arrow pointed north, making sure the compass's orienting lines ran parallel with the map lines. [If you do not have the declination pre-set on your compass you can save time by drawing "magnetic" lines on the map before heading out.]

4) Chris read out the bearing marked at the direction-of-travel arrow, making sure to ignore the compass needle.

5) Our faithful leader now had the bearing and pointed the way to camp.

6) While Chris was calculating the bearing on the topo map he took special note of the compacted contour lines (indicating a steep cliff to the north-west) marked alongside his penciled line. This landmark acted as a "handrail" to follow, making sure we were headed in the right direction.

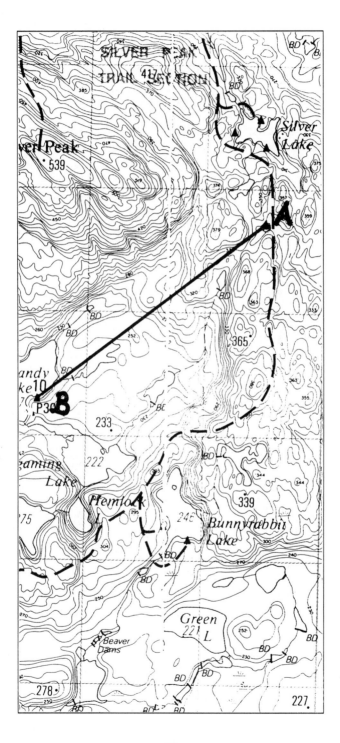

But What If You Don't Know Where You Are?

So far I have discussed ways to navigate when you know your exact whereabouts. But what if you're completely lost! You are on an island along the shores of Georgian Bay, but you have no idea which island. What do you do now? That's easy: just follow the rules of triangulation (see diagram):

1) From where you are standing you can recognize at least two outstanding landmarks, i.e., two high ridges in the distance.

2) Locate these permanent landmarks on your topographic map.

3) Take a field bearing on ridge A (181°), then on ridge B (153°).

4) By using the back bearing of each point (subtract 180 degrees from bearing, giving a back bearing of 354° for A and 326° for B), draw a line with the compass base-plate from ridge A and then from ridge B. Note: if your compass with a pre-set declination screw you must change your magnetic bearings to true north by reversing the declination rule before calculating your whereabouts on the map.

5) You're standing where the two lines bisect each other on the map.

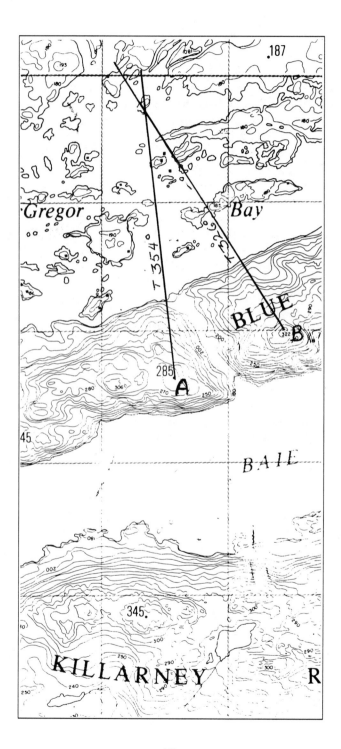

Nature's Direction Indicators

Forget what your Scout or Girl Guide leaders used
to tell you; moss does not grow on the north side
of the tree. It is true that moss likes the shade and
that the sun rarely shines on the northfacing slope;
but I've hiked through deep forested valleys where
the sun has a difficult time penetrating the upper
canopy and I've witnessed moss growing right
around the entire trunk. The problem with the moss
trick is that it is not accurate enough to depend on.

The only accurate direction indicators in nature
are the sun and the North Star.

To locate the North Star in the night sky, look
for the Big Dipper. Draw an imaginary line from
the two stars that form the lip of the dipper. The
line will point to the North Star, shining almost directly over "true" north. Instead of travelling at
night, mark the direction with a stick and wait until
morning.

It is possible to locate south by using an analog
watch, equipped with an hour hand. With the watch
in a horizontal position, point the hour hand toward
the sun. The halfway mark between the hour hand
and twelve o'clock is approximately south.

It is always best to carry along a map and a compass, but if you are in a desperate situation you'll
be amazed at the things you'll think of.

I once found my way out of the bush by spotting
a flock of gulls circling in the sky just ahead. Where
there are gulls there's garbage, and where there's
garbage there are humans.

Another time wildlife gave a helping hand to find
four children lost in the woods at night.

On my first night as residential supervisor at an
outdoor education center I did the routine head-
count at dinner and discovered, to my horror, that
somewhere in the surrounding 3000 acres of wood-
land, four special-education students were lost.

I gathered as much information as I could and
quickly divided the staff into search parties, equip-
ping each group with a walkie-talkie.

I chose to search the pine forest northwest of the Centre, as I was familiar with many of the animal trails the kids might have followed by mistake. With the sun sinking fast I knew it wouldn't take long for the four frightened kids to panic and scatter further into the darkened forest.

For over half-an-hour I jogged up and down whistling and yelling the children's names. With the sun minutes from setting I finally called in on my walkie-talkie and asked the staff to call the police, stating that we might have a night search on our hands.

As I sat on top of a rocky knoll, looking over the thick forest canopy, I noticed a flock of crows circling and calling above a small stand of pine, just west of the main highway. I remembered how crows, bluejays, and even red squirrels act as "guardians" of the forest. They call out an alarm the moment an outsider trespasses into their territory. "That's it!" I thought, "The boys are the trespassers."

I called the staff on the walkie-talkie and explained that I had found the lost boys just west of the highway and asked them to meet me there. I didn't even wait for a reply. Setting a compass bearing at the stand of pine I ran from the knoll, down toward the angered crows.

By the time I reached the stand of trees the sun had set and both the crows and the boys were nowhere to be seen. I questioned my "guardian of the forest" theory and walked out to the highway.

As I hiked up the ditch alongside the road, I saw, to my surprise, four lost boys being greeted by the Outdoor Center's staff, the police, and a very relieved homeroom teacher.

Chapter Five:

Bears, Bugs, and Beavers

Battling Bear-phobia

During the summer of 1992 I paddled solo the upper section of the Missinaibi River; the same summer when cloudy skies and cold temperatures were an everyday occurence, blueberry bushes failed to ripen, and irritable bears wandered the woods suffering from hunger.

Just two days before my trip, a young geologist working near the area was decapitated by a bear. Apparently the bear mistook him for a moose calf, a dietary option for the bruins when blueberry bushes become sterile from frost. Already stricken with bear-phobia, I took extra precautions when bear-proofing my camp.

Every night without fail I strung my pack up high on a rope hoisted between two trees or a strong outstretched branch. The sealed pack contained everything that held odors: food, utensils, water bottle, soap, sunscreen, and even toothpaste (the memory of catching a black bear munching on the minty Crest from its tube which he robbed from my pack

serves as a constant reminder). I also made sure to rid my camp of food smells by preparing meals well away from the tent site; I wore a seperate set of cooking clothes; and even went out of my way not to look anything like a moose calf.

Traveling alone I was lucky enough to spot wild-life on almost every bend of the river: nine bears in twelve days to be exact. On the Split Rock Falls portage the roar of the rapids and a howling wind deafened the clangorous singing I regularly bel-lowed out while on the trail to announce my pres-ence. As I crested a hill I suddenly met a startled bear. Immediately we both ran in opposite direc-tions and, if it wasn't for a heavy canoe balancing over my shoulders, I would have noticed the pine tree I ran into. Luckily the bruin was gone by the time I came to.

Most bears I encountered reacted by running away. It was only when I camped in the main camp-ground on route that I was harassed by what the park staff titled "nuisance bears." One large bear was so persistent in plundering at my food cache that I was forced to adopt a "mild aggression" tech-nique I learned in the more popular bear-infested Algonquin Provincial Park: I encouraged the bear to leave my camp by banging pots together, growling in a powerful deep voice and tossing the odd rock his way. One bit of advice: never aim directly at your target or he will attempt to show you who's boss (I have out-of-focus photos to prove it).

The trip down the Missinaibi River was an expe-rience that helped rid me of bear-phobia. It is im-possible to tell you how to react to a bear; each occurence is different and your reaction will depend on the particular circumstance. Just remember that you are only visiting where the bear resides. We must learn to accept that the presence of these ani-mals helps to define the term "wilderness" and we must never destroy this wild beast for acting out a characteristic we ourselves hold in common — being unpredictable!

Vampires Of The Forest

Being bitten by blackflies or the pesky mosquito can drive anyone "buggy." In fact, bug experts say that a person in the woods, without wearing protective clothing, could die from loss of blood in less than two hours as a result of blackfly and mosquito bites. But no one has been crazy enough to stand naked in the forest and allow themselves to be attacked by these midget vampires to prove the experts' theory.

Not many people have anything good to say about these bothersome bugs. But I think blackflies and mosquitoes are great; after all, understanding just what they're about does help make the itchy bites of these tiny insects a little easier to bear.

The blackfly is the first bug to show itself in early spring. Unlike the mosquito which lays its eggs on the smooth surface of a pond, marsh, or puddle, the blackfly lays its eggs in a running brook or river.

After hatching, the baby blackflies (larvae) drift downstream, holding on to a strand of silk like a spider to its web on a windy day. Once it finds a place to feed, the blackfly spins a disk-shaped pad of silk on a log, rock, or blade of grass; holds itself in place with its hooked rear end; and begins to snack on tiny bacteria, protozoa, diatoms, and even the odd brother and sister blackfly drifting by.

When the blackfly grows into an adult the bug pulls itself out of its old skin, stretches out its wings, rises quickly to the surface in a tiny gas bubble, and "pops" itself free. The males fly off to munch on plant nectar and the thirsty females search out a warm-blooded animal for a bloodmeal.

Neither the female blackfly nor the mosquito can develop her eggs without drinking blood.

It's amazing how the female blackfly is able to steal your blood. The blackfly actually slices your skin open with jagged mouthparts like a pair of sharp scissors. After the initial cut, other mouth-parts (called stylets) hold back the skin with tiny hooks while the blackfly snips again and again until it slices open your capillaries and tastes blood. She fills up with half a teaspoon (two milliliters) of rich blood.

You usually don't feel the blackfly cutting into your skin, but, after she finishes her bloodmeal, the female wrenches her head from side to side, trying to free the hooked mouthpart. Ouch! Now that part smarts. And this is why, when you feel the blackfly bite behind your ear and you swat it, blood smears down your neck.

Mosquitoes don't bite you like the blackfly, but they do suck your blood with a needle-like mouthpart, which pierces your skin. They spit saliva into the wound to stop your blood from clotting, fill their blood bank, and quickly pull out and fly away.

Female blackflies and mosquitoes are mostly attracted by body temperature, lactic acid produced by muscle movement, and carbon dioxide produced when you breathe out. They love warm sweaty skin on a cool day. Warm days, however, seem to confuse them. Both bugs also dislike pouring rain, cold days when temperatures reach below 30°F (10°C), and blowing winds; the blackfly in particular is not a strong flyer and can only reach a top speed of half-a-mile (one kilometer) per hour.

Dark colors attract blackflies and mosquitoes more than shiny bright colours. Wearing black pants (blue jeans are the worst) is not a good idea; lime green neither attracts them nor keeps them away; and hot pink pants work great!

Bug hats are an essential part of your equipment list in early spring. I remember a "city-slicker" that joined my regular canoe mates and me on an annual spring fishing trip in Algonquin Provincial Park. He thought bug hats were for sissies and decided not to take one along. On the first portage he ended up throwing his gear down on the path and running through the forest like a madman. We found him twenty minutes later, his entire body swollen with bites.

Out of all the bug repellents on the market the most commonly used is DEET (Diethyl Toluamide). The chemical is effective in keeping blackflies, mosquitoes, no-see-ums, and ticks away from your exposed skin, but read the warning on the label and see how effective it is on stripping paint and melting plastic. When I was working as a tree planter for the Ministry of Natural Resources in Northern Ontario we were told never to put the repellent on our hardhats. One worker ignored our supervisor and splashed it on. At the end of the day his yellow hardhat was black with layer after layer of dead bugs. To prove his point our supervisor took the hat and banged it against the side of his truck. The plastic headgear cracked right down the middle. Right then I began to ponder on the effects DEET had on skin.

Repellents containing citron like Avon's Skin-So-Soft hand lotion are more gentle to the skin and are almost as effective as DEET. Taking vitamin B tablets during the three months leading up to your trip is also said to be helpful. Eating lots of citrus fruit and garlic, and avoiding bananas are other suggestions to think about.

BEAVER FEVER

While guiding a school outing in early spring along the Silhouette hiking trail in the interior of Killarney Provincial Park, one of my students, forewarned about drinking untreated water, decided to take a cup full of "fresh" water slopping over a beaver dam. He was forced to acknowledge his foolish act when I caught him a few days later slumped over a log wondering why Montezuma had moved from Mexico to the northern woods of Ontario to seek his revenge.

More and more campers are finding themselves affected by, not Montezuma, but a tiny waterborn pathogen called Giardia Lamblia. Giardia cysts are deposited into bodies of water from the feces of infected mammals, especially that of beaver, hence the nickname of Giardia Lamblia sickness, "beaver fever."

It takes only ten Giardia cysts to infect your body. The microscopic protozoan, measuring 21 microns in length (the tip of a sewing needle measures 700 microns), hatches inside the small intestine with an incubation period from five days to several months, reproduces like wildfire, establishes a colony, and then has a little party inside your gut — making you sick as a dog.

Symptoms can be severe or completely unnoticeable. They include: diarrhea, abdominal cramps, fatigue, weight loss, flatulence, and nausea — not a pleasant experience while staying a week in the bush away from flush toilets and the local pharmacy store.

Of all the tiny "nasties" that can be found swimming in your water bottle, Giardia Lamblia is the most common, and luckily it is also the least dangerous. The protozoa Tularemia is a little more serious. It is similar to an infectious plague-like disease that infects man and more than eighty percent of other species of mammals. It is also caused by a bacterium, which gains entrance to the body and multiplies rapidly through the bloodstream, invading cells of the liver, spleen, lungs, kidneys, and lymph nodes.

When a person is infected by Tularemia they can expect the worst flu-like symptoms: a high temperature, headaches, chills, sweats, nausea, vomiting and body pains. Extreme symptoms, as if the others aren't bad enough, are as follows: swollen area where infection entered (hands, arms, face,or neck), inflammation of eye membrane,and general enlargement of the lymph nodes.

The parasitic protozoa can be transmitted the same as Giardia — ingestion of contaminated untreated water from either a carcass or the body discharge of an infected animal (mainly beaver and humans). It can also be given by innoculation from biting insects (blood-sucking flies, ticks, lice, or fleas). A very high percentage of trappers fall ill to this sickness due to their constant contact with the fur, internal organs, body fluids, and discharge of infected animals.

Apart from the above pathogenic protozoas, Giardia and Tularemia, there are many other varieties of bacteria floating around, depending on your whereabouts. E. coli gives you the trots, Kleisiella pneumoniae causes pneumonia, and the familiar Salmonella may give you food poisoning or infect the camper with a bout of typhoid fever.

Since there is no way of guaranteeing that even the most remote lakes and streams are free of "beaver fever," or surface-water pollutants like gas fuel, pesticides, and heavy metals from mines, you must either boil your drinking water, treat it with chemicals, or filter out the "nasties."

Boiling

It has always been said that you must boil your water for at least five minutes before it is safe to drink. Many campers find that boiling water for such a long period of time is a waste of stove fuel or simply too inconvenient just for a hot cup of tea. Since it only takes a low boiling point to kill most Giardia, bacteria, and even viruses, it is now acceptable to bring your water to a rolling boil before dipping in the tea bag.

Chemical Treatment

For years I brought along iodine tablets to purify my drinking water; I found the odor and iodized taste preferable to the bland taste of boiled water, not to mention the time saved if I wanted a cold drink while on the trail. However, the more I found myself out in the wilds using the tablets day in and day out, the more I questioned the small print on the bottom of the air-tight bottle: "use only for emergencies."

The iodine tablets kill both the bad bacteria in the water and the good bacteria living inside your intestine that help you digest.

For infrequent use, iodine tablets do save time. The dose is one tablet for every quart of water and wait for fifteen minutes; or two tablets if the water is cloudy or colder than 50°F (9°C) and then wait for one hour. If you dislike the taste of the iodine I suggest you disguise it by adding flavor crystals, such as Tang, to your drinking water.

You can purify water by passing it through filter purifiers such as those marketed by Water Technologies Corporation; the fine mesh filter contains iodine resin. The iodine is only released when there are micro-organisms present. The temperature of the water is irrelevant and your water doesn't get "spiked" with iodine unless it needs it. The disadvantage is knowing when to change the iodine-laced filters. If the water loses its strong iodine taste, it's safe to say you need a replacement.

Filters

Filters strain the clear clean water away from the solids but they do not neccessarily remove all the bacteria or viruses (both are small enough to go through the filter). They do remove cysts and the new carbon filters, such as First Need, eliminate chemical pollutants (you never know what a previous pulp-and-paper mill dumped nearby when environmental regulations weren't as stringent).

To ensure your filter works properly it is important to backwash it at the end of each day while out on the trail and to replace it once a year. Make sure, as well, that the water used to backwash the filter is purified.

Chapter Six:

Soggy
Survival

NATURE'S WEATHER FORECASTERS

During a weekend jaunt through a chain of lakes in the Haliburton Highlands, after believing weather reports of clear sunny skies, I was caught out in the open as a dark menacing cloud rolled in from the west, bombarding the blackened water with bolts of lightning like an Olympic javelin thrower.

Paddling blindly I made my way towards a small island, quickly erected my tent on a rocky knoll, and began to wait out Mother Nature's fury.

After hurricane winds snapped the tent's ropes and flimsy nylon walls, I huddled under the collapsed dwelling through the longest night of my life, angry at myself for being so unprepared.

The next morning, happy to be alive, I promised myself never to be caught off-guard again.

The incident forced me to quickly learn ways to survive a soggy night and at the same time lift my dampened spirits.

On an extended trip into the interior you usually don't have helpful reports from the weatherpeople. But don't panic; they're usually wrong anyway. Learn to depend on nature's clues. Learning to recognize telltale signs of an approaching storm will give you ample time to erect a shelter:

1) The old wives' tale of leaves flipping upside-down, showing their light-colored bottoms flickering in the breeze, is based on actual biological fact. The air temperature and wind direction alter before an approaching weather change.

2) Hordes of biting insects, especially mosquitoes, come out of hiding for a quick snack before they head for cover. Ants will construct tiny dikes from dirt piled up at the entrance to their tunnels before it rains. Bees

stay close to their hives before a rainfall. When crickets chirp away busily it usually means warm weather.

3) Insect-eating birds, like swallows, will chase their dinner closer to the ground just before a storm hits. They will also fly higher when rain is no threat. It is actually the insects who are being affected by the fair weather updrafts, but the birds are easier to watch.

4) All animals become very active just before a storm hits. Red squirrels are especially known to place a pile of cones on their front doorstep before the rain starts to fall.

5) Smoke from your campfire will hug the ground if a storm is coming. If it rises straight up, clear weather can be predicted.

6) Aristotle's pupil, Theophrastus of Eresus, is thought to have been the first to coin the phrase "Red sky in the morning, take warning/Red sky at night, sailor's delight." The red color is an indication of little moisture in the air; rain during the next twenty-four hours is unlikely.

7) Even though rainbows are usually spotted right after a shower, the saying holds true: "Rainbow in the morning, shepherds take warning; rainbows at night, shepherd's delight. Rainbow to windward, foul fall the day; rainbow to leeward, damp runs away."

8) If a jet airplane's trail persists for several hours, rain could arrive within one day. The trail will slowly spread out into a thin white veil. The jet's trail, made up of ice crystals, does not dissipate rapidly because the upper

atmosphere is moist — a telltale sign that a low-pressure system is on the way.

9) "If the sun is in its house, it's going to rain." Sun halos or a ring around the moon, called a "moondog," give meaning to this phrase and are good indicators of an upcoming rainfall.

10) And this last catchy phrase is also helpful: "When dew is on the grass, rain will rarely come to pass; when the dew is gone, rain will come before too long."

Reading The Clouds

Clouds, gigantic lumps of visible water droplets or ice particles, are another excellent way to predict the weather.

Low fronts include stratus, nimbostratus, and cumulonimbus. Stratus are grey clouds that have a uniform flat base and usually bring light rain. Nimbostratus are darker grey in color and usually bring much heavier rainfall. Those dark, almost black clouds, with flat bottoms and towering thunderheads (something like an upside down anvil) are called cumulonimbus They are a clear indicator of an approaching thunderstorm.

The middle grouping of clouds include altocumulus and altostratus. The altocumulus are made up of a sheet of white or grey cloudlets, sometimes formed in rows. The altostratus, striated and uniform in shape, spread across the sky in a thin grey layer. Both cloud formations tell of inclement weather, but with the altostratus you have at least twelve hours before it begins to rain.

Cirrus, cirrocumulus, and cirrostratus clouds form in high altitudes and are the least trustworthy forecasters. Cirrus are separate, scattered wisps and usually indicate fair weather unless they become bunched together, meaning rain may fall the next day. Cirrocumulus clouds form a thin rippled pat-

tern in the sky. They may grow perpendicularly throughout the day, and if the vertical growth does not disperse, a quick shower may follow. And last, cirrostratus, a transparent veil creating a halo around the sun, is a prime indicator of a warm front; if it leads an altostratus cloud formation, "refreshing" rain could come down in less than twenty-four hours.

PREPARE TO GET WET

Studying cloud formations, feeling the change in air temperature, or just having the old rheumatism starting to act up again are also simple signs to warn you of an approaching storm and give yourself time to prepare for the worst.

That is exactly what you do: prepare for the worst. Believe me, it becomes quite nerve-wracking to attempt to build a shelter when the storm has reached its peak.

There's nothing worse than trying to keep warm in a spongy sleeping bag or munching on soggy sandwiches. So attempt to keep your equipment dry, especially your sleeping bag, tent, clothes, sneakers, and, above all, your matches.

Rain Gear

Like the majority of outdoor enthusiasts, when the new high-tech "breathable" rainwear came out I went out and spent a small fortune in an attempt to stay dry. The first year it worked better than I imagined. But after a few muddy portages the old and dirty outerwear began to leak like a sieve.

For the money, a two-piece nylon rain suit coated with a thin layer of a neoprene rubber or several layers of polyurethane will keep you just as dry from the rain, but your sweat will have a difficult time escaping. The cheap nylon rain suits also fail when the coating begins to peel off. Despite their shortcomings, I've gone back to the inexpensive nylon suits and when the water starts finding its way in, I toss it and purchase another one.

Flame On A Stick

Apart from a dry shelter, the most important camping tool is the wooden match. You should never have to have to depend on the old Boy Scout manual and attempt to rub two sticks together. It's not as easy as it sounds.

To keep the matches dry don't bother buying expensive waterproof matches. There are many inexpensive ways to keep the dampness out: an old 35 mm film cannister, an empty shotgun shell, or match-heads dipped in melted wax, all work well.

Sometimes even the best homemade or store-bought waterproof match won't sputter a flame after a long day out in the cold rain, so a lighter in your pack serves as an excellent back-up.

Natural fire-starters are very helpful to ignite a flame in damp weather. Birch bark is the best: it will burn even when wet. Dry pine, spruce, or fir needles can be found under the lower limbs of big trees. You can also make fire-starters by melting wax and sawdust together or by burning a birthday candle.

Chapter Seven:

Bruises, Blisters, And Band-aids

Personal First-Aid Kit

I believe that prevention is a camper's best medicine, which is why half the items in my first-aid kit have yet to be used. I also believe that a standard first-aid course taken at night school along with a pocket-sized first-aid manual stuffed inside your pack is a lot better than someone like me trying to explain on paper skills that could mean life or death.

So, I have decided simply to list the twenty-five essential items that I include in my first-aid kit:

1. Nylon pouch or organizer — commercial first-aid kits are rarely equipped with all the essential items. To save money and to ensure you have exactly what you need, purchase your own lightweight organizer, available with a variety of pouches and containers, and visit the local drugstore to fill it with the appropriate contents.
2. Extra-strength Tylenol or its equivalent (for relief of headaches and aching muscles)
3. Caladryl (for bee stings and bug bites)
4. Antacid tablets
5. Laxative
6. Iodine
7. Antiseptic cream
8. Sunscreen
9. Lip balm
10. Hand lotion (your dry hands will thank me.
11. Mosquito repellent
12. Throat lozenges
13. Water-purification tablets
14. Band-aids (various sizes)
15. Gauze pads (various sizes)
16. Feminine napkin (for soaking up blood from cuts and scrapes)
17. Ace bandages (for sprained ankles or swollen knees)
18. Butterfly bandages
19. Moleskin (for blisters)

20. Tweezers
21. Small mirror (for inspecting eye injuries or a clean shave)
22. Adhesive tape
23. Safety-pins
24. First-aid manual (explaining everything from splints, treatment for shock, and CPR)
25. Extras — you will find that along with the essential items each camper will need to bring a few extra items for their own special needs. I pack an extra Ace bandage for my weak knees, ear drops for my sensitive ears, and antifungal cream for my athlete's foot that flares up now and then when my feet get wet. Some of my friends bring along various prescription drugs, a jar of multi-vitamins, allergy pills, and a bee-sting kit to battle an allergic reaction. If you are camping with children be sure to bring lots of extra band-aids.

Foot Care

With all the various modes of travel, it is our feet that mainly get us from point A to B. So you can imagine how easily an outing in the interior can quickly change when a simple blister becomes disabling.

To avoid blisters forming on your feet make sure your hiking boots fit well and they're well broken in before your trip. Avoid wearing wet boots or shoes on the trail. Shoes are best packed away for use around camp. Moccasins or sport sandals are also comfortable footwear after a long day hiking.

In case your boots fail and that little annoying blister starts to form, moleskin can save the day. This thin felt-like material has a very adherent backing and comes in sheets that can be cut to the exact size and shape of the blister. Make sure your skin is clean and dry before you apply it.

Another helpful product to pack away in your medical kit is Second Skin. It is available in strips and is conveniently packed in a resealable foil envelope. After cutting off a strip, the plastic peels off one side and the gel film is placed on the skin. It can be held in place by a larger piece of moleskin.

Clean, well-fitting socks are also essential on any trip if you want to keep your feet fresh, not to mention to rid your tent of foot odor which seems to linger, even after your boots are tossed out the front flap by your tent partner. A pair of socks per day is not excessive, as well as a couple of thick woollies to wear around camp with your sneakers.

Knee Problems

After five days of trudging through three feet of snow in the interior of Killarney Provincal Park years ago, I ended up with arthritis in both my knees — a condition I wouldn't wish on my worst enemy.

To my hiking companions my damaged knees are an asset; I can predict an upcoming rain storm with seventy-five percent accuracy. To me, however, it's made life a living hell!

Once you have damaged your joints it's next to impossible to return them to normal. So, prevention is the key word in avoiding knee problems.

When you are walking downhill you are actually falling forward. What keeps you upright and your knees from sagging is the action in the big muscle in the front of the thigh — the quadriceps. That's the one that feels like jelly when you relax after a long day on the trail and the muscles have a chance to stiffen up.

When walking with a pack strapped to your back you are creating five times the weight that applies force down on the knees, causing the kneecap to squeeze against the femur, or thighbone.

The kneecap or patella can be damaged by weak quadriceps. As it is the center of rotation for the knee, it is highly vulnerable to stress, especially if one is out of condition.

The better the muscles work, the better they guide the kneecap along the front of the knee. In return, the knee can withstand more pressure. The muscle knows what to do, but without the right conditioning, it does it haphazardly.

To condition your knees for hiking, it's important to choose the proper sport. To tune-up the quadriceps smoothly and consistently the knees have to be trained in an aerobic way; cycling, running, and cross-country skiing work great. Don't choose stop-and-go sports such as tennis, racquetball, or weight-lifting. In these sports, the quardriceps work in a sporadic and anaerobic way.

At the trail's head it is important to warm-up properly before starting out and again when you return at the day's end.

If damage does occur remember the acronym RICE (rest, ice, compression, and elevation). This will sooth the tendon and muscle unit. Stretching also helps a damaged muscle; a heel-to-butt excercise helps to stretch out an inflamed unit.

As the pain subsides, try an isometric exercise. Lie down and extend your legs straight out, then hold them at about 45 and, finally, at about 90. Whenever possible do at least fifty of these, holding each for a count of three.

Sounds like a lot of work, doesn't it? But believe me, after my unforgettable mishap in Killarney Park, an ounce of prevention can stop a lifetime of pain.

Orthopedic Problems For Paddlers

Being on the open water, paddling day after day, can push your muscles beyond their limit, especially just after spring thaw when your itchy paddle-hand rushes you out while your canoe muscles are still in winter hibernation.

One of the most common muscle injuries happens when canoeists constantly battle foam and froth on a river, causing pain to the wrist and forearm. The pain comes from too much stress placed on the muscles and tendons while you grip the paddle shaft too tightly.

To prevent injury it's recommended that you ease up on the paddle while flushing through the deadly whitewater. But let's be realistic. Keeping the wrist straight during the pull phase of the paddle stroke, however, can lessen the discomfort a great deal.

Shoulder injuries are also a common problem for canoeists. I once had to fight strong headwinds all day while on the Missinaibi River and, instead of making camp early, I stubbornly pushed on, straining both my shoulder muscles. I was forced to lay idle for three days. Once the injury has happened, all you can do is rest and apply ice and heat alternately to the injured muscle. To forestall stress on your muscles and joints, however, stretching exercises before heading out on the water, proper paddle strokes while on the move, or working out on the bench and military press prior to your trip,1 can be helpful.

Treating The Big Chill (Hypothermia)

During the spring, outdoor enthusiasts tread on very thin ice, so to speak, when they anxiously begin their annual trips along the northern waterways, unprepared for drastic changes in weather.

The dos and don'ts of treating hypothermia are an essential component of survival skills. The first thing to do is stay calm. Panicking in front of the victim only makes matters worse.

Wet clothing should be removed immediately because it conducts heat away from the body almost thirty times quicker than usual. If a sleeping bag is handy, place the victim inside.

Another person should disrobe and attempt to warm the person with their own body heat within the bag. This is not a time to become self-conscious; you are dealing with a life and death situation and I'm sure the victim will not mind.

Warm drinks can also be given, but make sure the victim is alert or the hot fluid will be sucked into the lungs instead of swallowed.

Advanced stages of hypothermia are frightening to both the victim and the first-aider, as the frozen body can become uncontrollably convulsive.

If other sources of heat, such as a campfire or cooking stove, are available, use them to heat the victim. Hot packs or the equivalent can also be placed over the major blood vessels in the neck, armpit, and groin.

For severe hypothermia the medical treatment is much more invasive. Cardiopulmonary resuscitation and cardiac massage must be given to a patient whose heart has stopped. This must be maintained until the patient is rewarmed and defibrillated. In the hospital, people have survived after hours of resuscitation efforts.

Do not resort to ancient remedies like rubbing snow on the exposed skin of the victim or forcing down alcoholic beverages (to either the victim or the first-aider); they just make matters worse.

Exercise great care if you have to move the hypothermia victim and never take any unnecessary risks with other lives. But, most of all, don't get discouraged.

What's more important than how to care for someone suffering from hypothermia is how to prevent it from happening in the first place. Experience, practised rescue techniques, preparing well for trips during the off season, and common sense are the most essential lifesaving ingredients to pack away to avoid experiencing the "Big Chill."

Chapter Eight:

How to be a "green" camper

HOME AWAY FROM HOME 108

HOME AWAY FROM HOME

Everywhere you look someone is telling you ways to be more environmentally conscious at home or at work. I'm not knocking this new awareness, but nobody seems to be giving as much time to the art of being a green camper as they are to being a green consumer.

Wildlands are more than just unspoiled environments: they provide a human experience demanding isolation. Therefore, there are two dimensions to the problem of low-impact camping: damage to the integrity of the land and injury to the wilderness experiences of others.

In the past, government agencies have banned the use of cans and bottles, insisted that campers use only designated camp sites, issued limited-use permits and handed out pamphlets lecturing, "Take only photographs and leave only footprints." But these caretaking actions always seem to come after the damage has been done.

Bearing in mind that it is not malice but ignorance or unawareness that is the root of the problem, we as campers and concerned citizens must change our attitudes to protect the future of our natural environment. Ask yourself "what do I absolutely need? How can I travel through the wilderness so that I leave as little impact on the land as possible?" Both questions are similar. I've found in the past that if my goal is to achieve light weight, then I usually have less impact. For example, a gas stove is much lighter than an axe.

Choosing A Campsite

Always keep in mind that it is best to choose a high-impact designated campsite than to create a new site. Never dig trenches around tents, or cut or break standing trees. Spread out while hunting for firewood.

Tents should be erected on bare rock devoid of any plant life. If you have to set the tent up on green

vegetation, bear in mind that fauna such as meadow grass can withstand being slept on much better than blueberry bushes.

When you take one last look as you pack for another day of travel, make sure that whoever comes here next will never imagine anyone had camped there the night before.

The Perfect Campsite

Choosing a campsite is like picking the perfect apple at the grocery store; every apple on display may be edible, but somewhere in the assortment of fruit exists an apple with the right shape, texture, and free of any bruises.

To a hiker in the backcountry, a site located near a water source and sheltered by a thick canopy of conifers is perfect. To the car camper at a roadside park, any designated site that is within walking distance of the beach and is downwind of the latrines is suitable. To the canoeist paddling in the interior, the perfect site to make camp has a neck of pines for protection from the wind, but is still enough in the open to snag a breeze and keep the bugs at bay. The point of rock should face west-southwest to catch the morning sun at its tip as well as the last rays as they sink behind the opposite shore. And the most important requirement on the checklist: the site must be unoccupied.

Ideally the essential requirements for any camper after a long day on the trail, highway, or chain of lakes is a level, sheltered area, equipped with a cleared, comfortable tent site. Before choosing a place to erect your tent, however, look at the surrounding topography. If it begins to rain through the night you don't want to wake up floating on your therm-a-rest.

With the new-age dome-style tents it is no longer neccessary to peg your tent down. However, during high winds and heavy rain, you may want to secure the tent, or especially the rainfly, to the ground.

This makes choosing rock outcrops for campsites not always the best choice.

Speaking of storms, make sure there are no dead trees or snags hanging high above in the canopy: a strong wind could provide a rude and painful awakening.

Waiting out rainy days cramped inside your tent playing games of cribbage or rereading Stephen King novels can be a nightmare. A 10 x 12 foot (3 x 3.6 meter) tarp, however, rigged up between two or four sturdy trees rooted in front of the fire ring where bread is baking in the hot coals, can transform a miserable wet day into the highlight of the trip.

Apart from all the physical features neccessary, it is important to remember that to some people a perfect campsite is a memorable campsite. Sigurd F. Olson said it best when he wrote "I may forget portages, rapids, and lakes, which merge into a nebulous montage of country traveled over, but there are some campsites that stand out vividly in my mind as special places remembered."

Washing Up

I've watched dozens of campers rinse off their greasy dishes by the shore after a breakfast of bacon and eggs, only to return ten minutes later to fill up their water bottles for the day! As a general rule washing dishes, and yourself, should be done at least 30 yards (30 meters) back from the shoreline, even when you use biodegradable soap. Greasy frying pans and sticky pots can easily be wiped cleaned with a handful of dried pine needles and sand.

Cat-holes And Treasure Chests

I can't stand dicovering a garden of toilet paper mounds in the back of a campsite. It ruins the entire trip. If there isn't a treasure chest or thunder box made available on the site, go back at least 50 yards (50 meters) from camp, turn up an inch (three centimeters) of soil and, when finished, stir your waste into the soil with a stick. Then cover the toilet paper and excrement with a thin layer of soil, just like your pet cat does at home in the litter box. In two weeks it will become perfect potting soil.

Feminine hygiene products should be either burned or carried out. If buried, wild animals will be attracted to the strong scent of the pheromones and dig them up, decorating the camp with them.

Today's camper should practise low-impact camping as closely as today's consumer practises the three Rs. The time is here to make cat-holes and gas stoves as revolutionary as green products and the blue box.

Fires Vs. Stoves

For cooking, a stove is faster, lighter, and maybe even safer than an axe in the pack. However, in many parks there is no available firewood at interior sites. But I must confess that at least two nights out of a one-week excursion I curl up around an evening blaze. I can't help it.

So why haven't I changed? I think we're simply reluctant to lose our identity with fire itself. It makes us feel secure and holds back the darkness. Slowly, however, I'm becoming more of a stove convert. I can tell of a few memorable nights of northern lights and star-gazing when the glare of an evening fire was absent from my site. Campfires should be considered luxuries, not necessities.

Chapter Nine:

Quest for Fire

BUILDING A CAMPFIRE 116

- Fuel
- Starting The Blaze
- It Still Won't Go

BUILDING A CAMPFIRE

The day my father handed me a match and asked me to light the evening fire was the day I became a full-fledged camper. Being allowed to participate for the first time in creating an essential ingredient to our backcountry ritual was an incredible stepping-stone for me.

Building a campfire is a work of art. First you must choose a proper site. If a designated fire ring has already been constructed, use it! If not, make sure to place the circle of rocks on level ground, and if there is no bare rock available then clear a three foot (one meter) radius or more free of dry twigs or exposed roots. Also make sure there are no dead trees or hanging branches with dry conifer needles at least twelve feet (four meters) directly above the fire site.

Fuel

Back in my days of Boy Scouts I was told again and again that an axe or hatchet is an indispensible tool for venturing out into the wilds, and to this day I can't understand why. Still, with my Scoutleader's teachings drilled deep down inside me, I continued

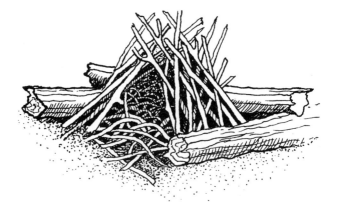

to store a small hatchet in the bottom of my pack for years, never once using it. Last year, however, while camped on a chain of lakes thirty minutes from my home, I pulled out my hatchet, blew off the dust, and began hacking away at a pile of birch logs previously cut by a camper with a lightweight chainsaw.

In my haste to get a warm fire going, my third swing of the hatchet glanced off the wood and embedded itself into the top of my right hand.

The cut didn't bleed right away, but by the time I unpacked my first-aid kit my hand was covered with blood. It took three changes of gauze and a role of surgical tape before the bleeding stopped, along with several Tylenol to control the swelling while I paddled out to my vehicle.

Needless to say I have since sold my hatchet at a garage sale and haven't missed it since.

If I were to choose any wood-cutting tool to pack along on an interior trip, it would be a folding lightweight saw. Camping companions have argued with me that an axe can do anything a saw can do, as well as hammer in tent pegs; the funny thing is, their dome-style tents aren't even equipped with tent pegs.

Even though I pack a saw, I seldom use it. I believe that all the dry dead wood neccessary for a good campfire can be gathered along the forest floor and broken over your knee.

Gather the deadfall ranging from finger to arm size, bundle it together, then drag it back to camp to be broken up in short lengths. To ensure the wood hasn't begun to rot or isn't still green, listen for a sharp snap when you break it in half.

Each tree species has an individual burning characteristic. Conifers (softwoods), such as pine and cedar, are excellent fire starters because they flare up quickly. When it comes to heat value, however, the flame is short-lived, creates dangerous sparks, and produces very few coals. Deciduous (hardwoods) are the best species for heat value. This dense, heavy wood keeps a long-burning flame with hot coals left behind for cooking. They are not as efficient for kindling. Sugar maple, white and yellow birch, and beech are some of the best, and most common, fuel for the fire.

Starting The Blaze

To start a fire think small. One of the biggest mistakes of first-time fire starters is to be too eager to produce a roaring blaze. Too much fuel too fast robs valuable oxygen and will eventually smother the fire.

Beside the fire ring place a heap of tinder (strips of birch bark gathered around the base of a tree, dry pine needles or grass, wood shavings, even fluff from a cattail's seedhead will do), a pile of dry softwood kindling no thicker than a pencil, two piles of finger-size kindling, a pile of arm-size hardwood, and then a separate mass of large logs — or "all nighters" as I like to call them.

First, place a row of arm-size hardwood in the fire ring to act as a base plate. Lay a handful of the dry tinder on top of the hardwood. Next comes the dry, pencil-size kindling, placed parallel over the tinder, approximately three inches (seven to eight centimeters) apart. In the opposite direction lay another row of twigs, finger-size. Now, while shielding the well- constructed pile of wood from the wind, light the tinder at all four corners with a wooden match or butane lighter. As the kindling catches flame, slowly feed the fire with the larger arm-size hardwood, making sure to keep a gap between the sticks to allow the fire to breathe.

It Still Won't Go

On a dry summer day it's usually quite easy to light a fire. But when it's wet and cold and a fire can become life-saving, it is next to impossible to ignite the fire ring. The key to start the fire burning, not smoking, is to add a make-shift fire starter. Flammable paste or fire sticks can be purchased at an outdoor store, but homemade fire starters are cheaper and work just as well. Rolled up newsprint soaked in paraffin works, as do softwood shavings mixed with wax in a dixie cup, cotton balls coated in vaseline, square pieces of rubber tubing, steel wool, or a stunted candle. Resin or pitch from conifer trees can also be collected around camp. This gum-like substance can be found next to wounds on the tree's bark or on balsam fir; the bark's boils or blisters can be squeezed like a pimple to get at the pitch inside.

Once the campfire is lit it's time to celebrate, gather around for warmth, cook a hot meal, tell a joke or a tall tale, keep the night at bay, or sit around the glowing flames and chat about the meaning of life.

Chapter Ten:

Cold Camping

OUT IN THE COLD 122

OUT IN THE COLD

A day hike or ski in the winter months can be quite refreshing, but to some the idea of sleeping in the frozen woods is totally insane. I remember my first winter overnight and even though I was hooked on "cold camping" after the initial ordeal was over, I questioned my sanity the moment the sun set below the tree line. Bitter cold suddenly clamped down on the forest like an unrelenting bully; the stillness and seclusion of the cold night air haunted me.

I chose a thick stand of pine to spend the night. I erected my tarp, placed my sleeping bag over a bed of hemlock boughs, and, with numbed hands, scratched a match to life on my belt-buckle to start my evening fire.

Slowly the flames matured and warmth returned, followed by an uncomfortable tingling sensation as my body began to unthaw.

Smoke steamed up into the night sky as I dined on beef stew and helped myself to a cup of Irish coffee. Within my shelter, wrapped to withstand the below-zero temperatures, I felt wealthy, safe, and contented.

Admittedly, there are a number of hazards that go along with trekking through a frozen landscape and I strongly believe winter camping is not for everyone, but if you pack along the essentials (a little insanity included) and choose to head out between late February and early March when sub-zero temperatures are not the norm, your first excursion could be like a day at the beach.

Fashions You Can't Freeze In

Keeping in mind that your body heat is what actually keeps you from freezing, the type of clothing you wear is crucial. But before you go out and spend your life savings on up-to-date fashion wear, remember that old-time trappers and explorers survived the cold without the aid of Gore-tex.

The trick is to dress in layers. Start off during the cold morning looking like a walking puffball if you wish, but as you generate heat through exercise, peel off the layers to avoid your sweat freezing to your skin. The outer layer should not be the main insulator; save that job for the bulky wool sweater or fleece and synthetic long underwear. The "breathable" outerwear (jacket and pants) should protect your body from the cool wind, and it should have an assortment of zippers to allow quick ventilation.

A foot wrapped in ten pairs of socks and then squeezed into a tight-fitting boot will freeze due to poor blood circulation. You can lose up to one-third of your body heat through your head so, without meaning to sound like an over-protective parent, make sure to wear a hat. The traditional woollen toques or the new softer Polarplus beanies work well, but in extreme cold temperatures balaclavas, made from the same material as your long underwear, are preferred. Neck gaiters made from Polarplus fabric helps to seal the gap between collars and caps.

To keep your fingers from freezing it's best to wear mittens instead of fingered gloves. Moose hide mitts are all right until they get wet, but the new mittens composed of a Gore-tex shell and fiberpile or Thinsulate insulation will keep your hands warm even when coated in ice.

On And Off The Trail

While on the trail or sitting around camp make sure to eat lots of calories; winter camping is no time to go on a diet. Stop frequently to boil a quick cup of hot tea to warm your insides. You will rarely have difficulty staying warm during the day on the trail, but the night air brings a bone-numbing chill. The moment you finish setting up camp, change into a dry pair of long underwear and socks. I keep my extra dry clothes in the front pouch of my parka so they are nice and warm to put on.

Choosing Where To Sleep

Daylight is shortened during the winter months and it usually takes over an hour to set up camp, so be prepared to end the day on the trail early.

Avoid making camp on designated summer sites; with the heavy use they receive throughout the prime season they are usually far too exposed. Choose a well-protected wooded area, away from the wind and blowing snow. Before setting up camp, stomp down the snow with your snowshoes to compact it.

You have four main choices of shelters to sleep under. You can choose to drag a durable canvas prospector's tent and a portable pot-belly stove behind you on a wooden sled, but that would be too easy. Most cold campers choose a four-season nylon tent, extra large for plenty of gear. If you wish, however, you can dig a snowcave, and line it with a plastic tarp — it's cozier than you think! You can also construct a simple tarp shelter in front of a warm fire and a makeshift heat reflector, and line your bed with a plastic tarp or some carefully chosen hemlock boughs. As long as you don't forget to wake up every hour or two to feed the fire, you'll stay snug on top of a carpet of snow.

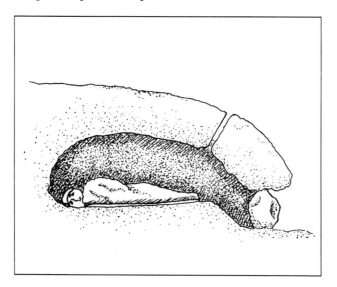

Snowshoeing

Tommy Baker, the class bully, used to tease and taunt me throughout public school for being bow-legged. For quite a while his relentless joking, — "Hey Callan, where's your horse?" — used to really bother me; that is, until that magical day during gym class when Mr. Finnigan, our phys-ed teacher, introduced our class to the art of snowshoeing.

As we spent the morning walking around outside with the snowshoes lashed to our feet, I realized that by being bow-legged I had an advantage over the rest of my classmates. Just before the end of the two-hour period, Mr. Finnigan announced a snow-shoe race across the football field. Bow-legged Callan beat little brat Baker and the rest of the class to the finish line!

You don't have to be bow-legged to snowshoe, but it sure does help. A booted foot would plunge

straight through the surface of snow without these handy helpers.

When going to purchase your pair of snowshoes don't worry too much about the model. Be more concerned with the style of the shoe itself.

For walking across flat, semi-open terrain the proper style of snowshoe to use is the Michigan model or what I prefer to call the Algonquin snowshoe. It is shaped like a teardrop with its tail lagging behind to track a straight line and keep the tips out of the snow.

In hilly or mountainous areas, the standard bear-paw style is more commonly used. With no tail it's easier to walk. I also use the bear-paw in early spring for walking through deep, crusty, corn snow.

The other two main styles of snowshoes are the Ojibwa and the Alaskan. The Ojibwa is used for open country, with its long length and upturned toe giving extra support and stability. The shoe's tip is

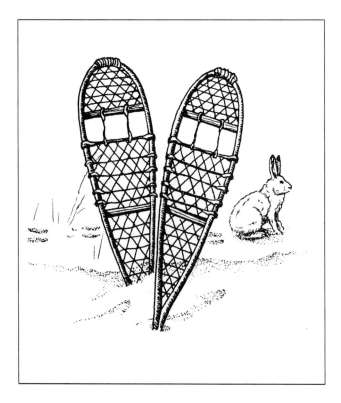

different from other styles because it is pointed like the back-end of the Michigan style. The Alaskan is quite similar to the elongated Ojibwa, except the toe is rounded like all the rest.

All these are made from wood. Outdoor stores, however, are now carrying a variety of new light-weight plastic or anodized aluminum styles equipped with mini-crampon bindings for traveling across packed snow or ice. Personally I still pack an old wooden pair of snowshoes I purchased at a garage sale. I find the cheap plastic shoes are exactly that — cheap, and the aluminum style are far too expensive for my liking.

Through years of experience, I have found out the hard way that during a bitter cold day when you are forced to free your hands from clumsy warm mittens so you can once again adjust the apparatus which holds your feet to the snowshoe, it is the bind-

ing that becomes more important than the shoe style.

I could write endlessly on types of snowshoe bindings, from the simple squaw hitch to a piece of old inner tubing. To keep it short and simple, the most common binding consists of a simple combination of a wide toe-peice and a leather-heel strap with a cross strap over the instep.

After the binding comes the boot. Oil-tanned moccasin boots worn with one light pair and one heavy pair of wool socks are great for snowshoeing. A winter camping companion raves about his pair of moccasins with the upper section of the boot made of thick canvas material. He purchased them from a native living in the far north where the snow is dry and crisp. In wet snow, however, his feet soon become wet; adding more oil just makes his sweaty feet unable to breathe. I've tried an assortment of footwear while snowshoeing but I always seem to resort to a good old pair of felt-lined boots with rubber bottoms and leather tops. They're on the heavy side, give me blisters, and at times can be too warm to wear, but with an extra pair of interchangeable liners in my pack I haven't lost a toe to frostbite yet.

I'll leave the tips on snowshoeing techniques to the experts (Osgood and Hurly's *The Snowshoe Book* is a great guide), but here is something you should keep in mind before taking your first steps. Walking with snowshoes lashed to your feet is little different than strolling down the sidewalk with sneakers, except the width of the snowshoe forces you to swing each foot around in a semi-circular motion. Being bow-legged makes the swinging a little easier — just ask my pal Tommy Baker.

Chapter Eleven:

Canoe Camping

CHOOSING YOUR CRAFT

My first canoe was an old beat-up fiberglass tub adorned with more patches than a pair of bluejeans from the sixties. I found it while working for a kids' camp. One day the other counsellors and I were given the duty of dumping half-a-dozen used and abused fiberglass canoes to make room for a new fleet of aluminum Grummans. It was either the garbage dump or my truck rack for "Gertrude," the least damaged of the lot.

Granted I have graduated to a more fashionable model for major trips. But when the mood strikes me I'll drag Gertrude from the backyard shed to take her out for a paddle. I'll be honest: she's not much to look at, even after a new paint job, but I'm amazed how shocked people are to see an avid canoeist like myself paddling such an eye-sore. I simply laugh off their teasing gestures, knowing that Gertrude has a major advantage over their fancier boats — she was free of charge.

With the price of canoes constantly rising you might want to search out the dump first before heading to the outdoor shop to purchase your first canoe. If you have no luck picking through the garbage, however, here is a breakdown on the different designs and materials used.

First, there is no perfect canoe. Some canoes, like the Prospector model, can do everything adequately: travel safely across a windy bay, hold a month's worth of supplies, or fight foam and froth on a wilderness river. But there is no canoe built that does everything really well. In a perfect world an avid canoeist would have a backyard cluttered with an assortment of canoe designs and makes. And just as a golfer chooses the best club to get the ball to the green, so the canoeist would choose the appropriate boat for the type of water they've planned to paddle that day.

Since it's difficult enough to scrape up the funds to purchase one canoe, the only reasonable solution is to go shopping for a canoe that suits your all-around character out on the water. Allow me to borrow from the experience of the We-no-nah Canoe Company: "For a canoe that you'll be happy with, choose a hull that is as long as possible given the limits of your size and the tightness of the corners you'll turn; pick as slim a hull as possible that still feels secure upright; and get a hull that's no deeper than needed for the gear you'll carry and the waves you'll cross."

Canoe materials are just as varied as their designs. It's hard to believe that the choice of materials used in construction of a canoe started with a walk in the bush. Now it seems everything is done in the science lab.

Weight and strength are the two major factors to consider when choosing the material to construct a canoe. Some materials create an almost indestructible canoe but are back-breaking on the portage; others are light as a feather but are as brittle as a potato chip. Here are some of the choices on the market.

Wood

Living in Peterborough, the birthplace of the modern canoe, I've been told by many traditionalists that a canoe is made of wood and canvas and a boat is made from anything else. Even though wooden canoes are expensive, require far too much maintenance, and are more fitting for a showcase than a wild river, I must say it feels wonderful to paddle one.

Aluminum

The aluminum canoe, or what some people call the Grumman canoe, is mostly used for institutional use as it is durable and inexpensive. However, the Grummans lack the aesthetics of a wood and canvas canoe, they are "pigs" on the portage, and, if the blade of your paddle hits the gunwale, the echoing bang sends every animal into hiding. In fact some local Peterborough paddlers I know think that people owning these institutional boats should be institutionalized themselves!

Plastics

Royalex is a type of plastic material consisting of a foam core sandwiched between sheets of ABS (Acrylonitrile Butadiene-Styrene) with a vinyl surface. It's strong and flexible, making it the obvious choice for whitewater canoeists. Just pray the river you're running doesn't have too many lengthy portages; Royalex boats weigh a ton.

Fiberglass and Kevlar

The most common fabrics used for canoe construction are fiberglass and kevlar. Fiberglass is a moderately tough boat, made up of either strips of cloth or chopped glass mixed with resin and then sprayed into a mold.

Some fiberglass models are superb and some are a joke.

Kevlar is much more expensive than fiberglass but is much lighter to carry and has added strength. Some manufacturers make up their own secret recipe of mixed fiberglass and kevlar. But buyer beware; make sure you don't get swindled by any sales reps that don't know their stuff.

What's my dream boat, you ask? If I had my choice of three canoes to store in my backyard I'd choose a fiberglass Kevlar 16 foot (5 meter) Trippercanoe for my week-long tandem trips in Algonquin or the Missinabi River; a lightweight Kevlar Soloboat for spending time alone in Killarney Provincial Park; and good old Gertrude for going anywhere and everywhere and basically doing whatever I please.

PERSONAL FLOATATION DEVICES (PFD'S): KEEPING YOUR HEAD ABOVE WATER

All right, I'll admit it; there are times when I've been caught canoeing across calm waters with my PFD (Personal Floating Device) tucked under my butt for extra comfort rather than zipped up on my body. After all, life jackets can do more than just keep one's head above water. The foam-filled vests make excellent seat cushions.

But there's one thing for sure, the moment the slightest breeze blows across the lake or I hear the roar of rapids up ahead while river paddling (especially if I plan to run, line, or wade them), my PFD quickly becomes a second skin.

Being caught dead without a PFD, however, seems to happen too often to canoeists. I remember hearing about a canoeist who had drowned while running the Albany Rapids on the Missinaibi River, just a year before I attempted the same run and overturned without mishap. The difference was, he wasn't wearing his lifejacket.

PFD Shopping Guide

When purchasing a PFD the most important point to remember is to buy one that is comfortable. At times I've worn my lifejacket on the river all day and then, without realizing, kept it on while sitting around camp. And in fact, during many spring trips I have worn my lifejacket as a second layer, simply to keep the chill out.

There are various models to choose from when shopping for PFDs. Stay away from the old-fashioned horse-collar types. They may keep your head above water, but they're uncomfortable, bulky, and not designed at all for canoeists. The vest-type jackets the Coast Guard label as a type III are the most widely used by avid paddlers.

Remember not to determine your choice directly on the flotation rating. A young child may need as much flotation as an adult. Think more of your body type than your weight. People with less body fat need more flotation. The average weight of an adult in water is 10 to 12 pounds (4.5 to 5.5 kg), so obviously a 140 pound (64 kg) man does not need 140 pounds @ kg) of flotation.

Plastic zippers are better than metal for wear and tear, especially if sand sticks inside the teeth. Ties and straps are great to have, but only as secondary fasteners. If the PFD is equipped with buckles as fasteners, make sure they are Fastex plastic buckles; anything else can be easily damaged when bumped around rocky rapids.

The perfect PFD should fit snugly, but not tightly to your body. A simple in-store test is to go shopping dressed in your canoe clothes, zip up a lifejacket, and do the following: 1) Grab the back of the PFD and wrench it upwards. Look side-to-side. Are you looking over your shoulders or is the PFD all you can see? If it's the PFD, then the lifejacket is too big. 2) Sit on the floor and pretend to paddle down the aisle. If the PFD chafes under your pits try another size. 3) Now check to make sure the zipper doesn't touch your chin.

The best test you can do before heading out on your trip, however, is to jump into the water while wearing your PFD. If it works and you're able to swim in it, great. If it doesn't then take it back to the store and keep shopping.

UP THE CREEK WITH THE RIGHT PADDLE

Whether you are prying your canoe into an eddy, slipping across calm flatwater, or slicing the bow through deep troughs, it's imperative that you are gripping the right paddle for the job.

There are various blade styles, each shape molded for the character of the canoeist as much as for the water course itself. The ancient Beaver Tail design, made from a single piece of maple or ash, is rounded at its tip and is perfect for creating the J-stroke across flat open water. For solo paddling, however, I prefer the much more slender blade with a shorter shaft, made from either ash or cherry.

For whitewater paddling you need a wide, square-tipped blade with reinforced tips to protect it from rocks. For capital control the top of the paddle should have a T-grip or the more comfortable soft T-grip if you want to use the paddle for flatwater as well. Many avid whitewater canoeists use the high-tech synthetic paddles made from fiberglass, graphite, kevlar, and plastic. No doubt they are tough paddles, but they're ugly and take away the whole mystique of paddling. A laminated softwood paddle works just as well if you look after it.

As for the new bent-shaft paddle, some people love it, and some hate it. A canoe intructor I work with, Al McKenzie, is a faithful user of the bent-shaft paddle. Interested to see what all the fuss was about I agreed to join him while he was teaching a group of students the benefits of using the bent-shaft.

Al started off by explaining how first-time canoeists automatically attempt to travel in a straight line by constantly switching their paddle from one side to the other. Paddling with a bent-shaft allows that natural reaction, with the stern paddler hollering out the command "Hutt" to indicate the right moment for both paddlers to switch sides, allowing the canoe to stay on track.

Al then displayed how at the end of a stroke with a straight paddle, water is pushed up to the surface, slowing your progress. When a bent-shaft paddle surfaces, the blade is vertical; no water is pushed up, no speed is lost, and less energy is used. This allows the canoeist to travel much further with less energy.

After watching the students trying out the new-fangled technique, it became obvious that paddling with a bent-shaft was quicker to learn than attempting the traditional straight-blade paddle strokes.

Everything Al said made perfect sense. But when he offered me a good deal on a pair of bent-shaft paddles at the end of the day I began to caress the flat wooden blade of my well-worn hand-crafted traditional paddle and politely responded, "Not in a million years!"

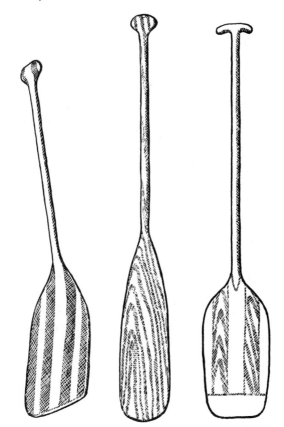

BASIC PADDLING STROKES

The Forward Stroke

The idea behind the forward stroke is quite simple: position the paddle far forward and then plunge the blade into the water, pushing water back and the canoe forward. But after an hour of paddling this "simple" forward stroke, your arms will begin to ache and you'll wonder if you're ever going to get to the end of the lake.

To make the stroke more effective and produce more power with the least amount of strain possible, make more use of your stronger upper-body muscles as opposed to your arms. This can be accomplished by twisting your torso, making the arm and shoulder on your paddling side extend as far ahead as possible and your body leaning slightly forward at the hips. Keep an eye on the position of your arms; the lower arm should almost be straight and your upper arm somewhat bent.

It is also important to note that while completing the stroke your lower arm should not go past your hip. If it does, you are wasting time and energy by actually lifting water up and pushing your bow down — similar to easing down on the brake of a car after depressing the gas pedal.

Back Stroke

The first stroke I learned while running rapids was the back stroke. It's the exact opposite of the forward stroke and is used to slow your canoe down instead of pushing it forward; something that may be crucial to know if you're headed straight for a rock.

The J-Stroke

During my earlier days of paddling I kept the canoe travelling in a straight line by twisting the paddle blade in toward the canoe, treating the paddle somewhat like a ship's rudder. At the time it made more sense to me than twisting it away from the canoe in the shape of a "J". Then I went tripping with Steve, an old friend and avid canoeist. The moment he put me in the stern and saw my "Goony" stroke he began to laugh hysterically: "You haven't got into that old bad habit, have you?" my friend asked. "We might as well be pulling an anchor with that water you're pushing back." It took a week out together, with Steve forcing me to change over to the proper J-stroke, before I realized how more efficient the "J" really is over the "Goony."

As the canoe moves ahead during the forward stroke, it will start to turn slightly away from your paddling side. But if you twist the paddle blade out from the canoe near the end of the forward stroke, forming the "J", the canoe will be forced back on course. Look at your upper wrist after completing the stroke to make sure you're doing it correctly; if your thumb is pointed down you just did the J-stroke and if it is pointed up you're back to doing the "Goony."

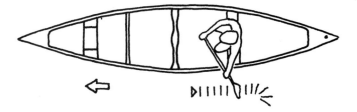

The Draw

The advantage of the draw is to be able to move your canoe effectively sideways and away from approaching obstacles. It is therefore no surprise that the bow person's job is to become proficient with this particular stroke. And it seems that the job of the person in the stern is to constantly yell out the command "Draw...draw!" every time the bow of the canoe heads directly for a sharp rock.

To produce a proper draw stroke place the paddle on the side you want to travel with the blade parallel to the canoe. By reaching outwards, plunge the blade into the water and push the water toward the canoe. When the paddle reaches the canoe take it out of the water and repeat the process. Once you become proficient with the stroke, you can advance by keeping the blade in the water after it has reached the canoe, turn it perpendicular, and knife it through the water to repeat your draw.

The Cross Draw

The cross draw is done in the bow only and is used when the bow person wants to draw on the opposite side they are paddling on without switching hands. Pivot at the waist, bring the paddle over to the other side of the canoe (do not change your grip on the paddle), and draw.

The Pry

The pry or pryaway stroke is similar to the draw, except instead of pulling the paddle blade toward the canoe you pry it away. If prying on the same side of your draw, you can alter the direction of the canoe without switching paddling sides.

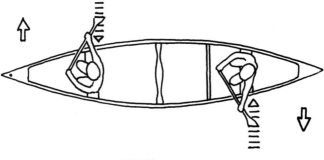

DRAW

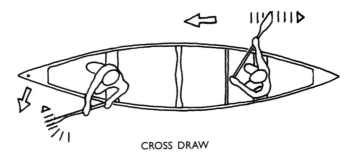

CROSS DRAW

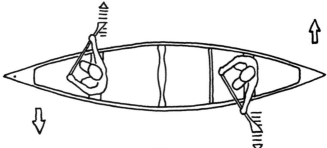

PRY

The Forward and Backward Sweep

The forward sweep turns the canoe away from your paddling side. Place the paddle blade parallel to the canoe and, with the shaft at an almost horizontal position, sweep the paddle wide in an arc. The more forward you begin the sweep and the further you end it will determine the turning effect of the stroke.

The backward sweep is the exact opposite of the forward sweep and moves the canoe in the opposite direction.

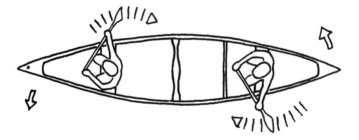

Combination Of The Draw/Pry/Sweep

When canoeing in tandem you can combine all three strokes (draw, pry, and sweep), to effectively move the canoe sideways to the left and then to the right or rotate on an axis 360 degrees in either direction.

SKULLING DRAW

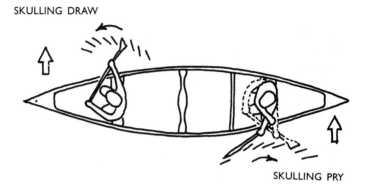

SKULLING PRY

ALL ABOARD!

Heading across a calm lake without tipping over in your small temperamental canoe is quite easy if you follow basic safety precautions by properly positioning your weight and not attempting to stand up suddenly and dance a jig. It's getting in and out of your canoe from dry land without falling in the drink that's the difficult part.

To get off to a good start from a dock, remember to keep your body low and place your weight in the center of the canoe. Because the canoe is much wider and more stable at the bow, the bow paddler enters the canoe first. While the stern paddler holds the canoe steady, sit on the dock alongside the canoe and place one foot into the canoe, positioning just forward of the seat on the keel line. Then, keeping your body as low as possible, place your hands on the gunwales and slowly bring your other foot into the canoe. Your partner now repeats the process in the stern while you hold the dock to steady the canoe.

If you are boarding from a beach or along a rocky shoreline place the canoe into the water with the bow pointing perpendicular to the shore. With the tip of the stern resting on shore have your partner hold the back of the canoe to keep it steady as you step along the centerline to the front of the canoe, keeping your body low and your hands firmly on the gunwales. Now your partner enters the canoe by placing one foot on the centerline, in front of the seat, then pushes off from shore with the other foot, continuing to keep their weight on the centerline while positioning themselves. Then away you go, dry sneakers and all.

PLAYING THE PART OF MR. CANOE HEAD

I once wrote a story in my local newspaper entitled "Portage to Hell." The account described in detail the grueling chore of walking along an extremely lengthy path through the woods with a hefty canoe balancing unevenly on my shoulders. Nowhere in the article did I mention where the particular portage was, yet in less than a week I began receiving mail from readers attempting to guess its whereabouts. One letter proposed it was the steepest portage in Killarney Provincial Park nicknamed the "Pig." Another guessed the legendary Greenhill Portage found along the wild Missinaibi River. Another likely contender was the unbelievable three-mile (5300 meter) portage from the Opeongo's East Arm to Dickson Lake in Algonquin Provincial Park. The "Pig" was the winner, but thinking back to the description of the "Portage To Hell," it could just as well have been any one of the other portages mentioned.

All paths leading from one lake to another or navigating around a set of rapids holds certain characteristics that canoeists curse about at the end of every trip: slippery rocks, steep inclines, bug-infested hollows, strained muscles, wrong turns, and that particular individual in the group who never seems to carry their share of the load. In fact the only thing paddlers seem to like about portages is the moment when the color blue can be seen ahead through the thick green forest, indicating the trail's end is near.

If you want to canoe, however, you must soon realize portaging is a way of life. The trick is to make the ordeal go as fast and easy as possible. If you are lucky, some enthusiastic students working the summer for the government will already have been on the route before you, clearing the debris fallen during the winter, and cutting back the new vegetation. If that's the case, the canoe can be carried overland first; but if the trail is poorly maintained scout ahead with the packs.

A few years back, my high-school friends and I had more brawn than brains. My regular canoe partner and I would strap on our heavy packs, lift the canoe onto our heads, and attempt to carry the paddles and PFDs in one hand, balancing the canoe with the other. The technique worked well for the first thirty feet (ten meters) or so.

The ultimate portaging technique when traveling tandem is to have one person carry the packs while the other shoulders the canoe. This way the portage can be done once. But don't feel inadequate if you have to go back for that extra load. The trip back is a prime opportunity to view the scenery you just struggled through blindly.

A paddling partner, Scott Roberts, designs bridges for a living and for years he has used his engineering background to explain how illogical it is to carry a canoe solo. He's even sketched out mathematical diagrams in the sand to prove his point. The proof is in the pudding however: once I allowed him to get his own way and attempted to carry the canoe tandem. It only took a few minutes of us shifting to opposite sides and bouncing the canoe off each other's heads before he threw the craft down and prepared himself for my "I told you so" statement. Believe me, one-person carries are easier in the long run.

To solo carry a canoe it is important that your canoe is equipped with a yoke; forget the traditional pair of paddles lashed across the thwarts or the uncushioned aluminum bar. A yoke is properly mounted when the canoe is slightly tail heavy. A tumpline attached to the inwales of the canoe is an added bonus, allowing you to shift the weight of the canoe from your shoulders to your neck.

Balancing the canoe on your shoulders is the easy part of portaging; it's getting the craft off the ground that takes a little practice. Start by standing amidship, grasping the gunwale with both hands and tilting the canoe so the hull is pressed against your legs. Now, by grabbing the center of the yoke with your right hand, hoist the canoe up on to your thighs. With the canoe resting on your thighs reach over and grab the far gunwale with your left hand, just forward of the yoke, and transfer your right hand from the yoke onto the gunwale nearest to you, just behind the yoke. The next part is the most difficult. Begin swinging the canoe gently back and forth on your thighs like a pendulum and then with one solid motion flip the canoe over your head with the yoke placed on your shoulders. Don't worry, your shoulders have the ability to locate the yoke on their own. Make sure you don't hesitate. The weight will lessen the faster you flip. Remember right-left-right-flip and you'll be fine!

At the trail's end, place the canoe "gently" down by using the opposite procedure, making sure to lower the canoe onto your thighs first to avoid smashing the hull against the rocky ground.

If you find it impossible to do a one-person lift, have your canoe partner lend a helping hand. Both of you lift the canoe by using the right-left-right-lift technique, but position yourselves in front of the bow and stern seats. Now, with your partner hoisting up the bow with their arms outstretched and the tail end of the canoe touching down on the ground, shuffle your hands along the gunwales until your shoulders fit under the yoke. Once you are nice and snug your partner can let go and begin the "Mr. Canoe Head" jokes while you go forth in search of that speck of blue at the other end of the "Portage To Hell."

REFLECTIONS ON RIVER RUNNING

For years I avoided river tripping like the plague. I enjoyed the relaxed atmosphere of paddling solo across a calm quiet lake far too much to get messed up with a group of over-enthusiastic river rats who wanted to play in rapids all day.

But recently I decided to see for myself what all the fuss was about. The moment the current took hold of my bow and began dragging me down river, I was hooked.

River running is totally different from canoeing along a series of connecting lakes. The river takes you on a voyage, gently floating you on its back one minute and then thrashing like an unbridled horse the next. Like many before me, my first battle with rapids was the biggest blooper of my paddling career. At the last minute one of my friends asked me to stand in for his regular bow partner during an annual whitewater race in southern Ontario. Neither of us knew enough to run rapids safely, but we pushed off from the starting point just the same.

Throughout the day we ground over gravel, splashed through haystack waves, and allowed every bend in the river to surprise us with its variety of boulder gardens and chutes. We even traveled down backwards after our canoe hit a rock and spun around. Thinking back, it was purely luck that we survived the whole ordeal, not to mention the fact that we went home with second prize.

I've learned from my experience, however, and the days are gone when I'd find myself blindly heading straight for foam and froth. It has now become a ritual for me to scout every rapid before attempting it. And before running the first chute I back-paddle constantly to slow my approach, watching for upstream vees which indicate submerged rocks and heading for the safety of downward vees which indicate a clear path. I also keep in control by practising effective strokes (draws, cross draws, prys, and ferry techniques) and by taking advantage of eddies so I can nestle in the calm before planning my next strategy.

To classify the difficulty of whitewater, Roman numerals are used (Class I being a breeze and Class V suicidal). Or you can guess the reasoning behind the names given to the rapid by previous river runners, such as Hell's Gate and Suicide Run.

To know its true power, however, you cannot label a rapid with a number from an International Scale or nickname it after Lucifer; a canoeist must get a three-dimensional view of the river by being swallowed up by it. This can't be properly done by filling in for a friend just before a race and hoping you'll survive. You must practise with the experts who can read a rapid like a book and teach the safe approach to paddling in whitewater. Only then will you truly understand the addictive feeling every canoeist gets the moment your boat is at the brink up the run and you suddenly realize that there's no turning back — you are now at the mercy of the river gods.

The Front Ferry

Picture yourself paddling down a northern river such as the Little Abitibi. The twenty-year-old map that you are following marks a portage on the right bank of the river just before a dangerous set of rapids. As you creep along the right shoreline to a point a few hundred meters upstream of the roaring whitewater you discover that the map is wrong. The portage is on the opposite side of the river. What do you do?

The only safe way to reach the portage is to "ferry" your canoe across the current a safe distance upstream from the dangerous section of river. The trick is to point your canoe at an angle upstream and tending toward the opposite shore. Powerstroke against the current and keep your canoe at an angle and the force of the river should move you straight across the river. If you find yourself having to paddle harder than you can, adjust the angle of the canoe. Stronger currents require sharper angles of attack.

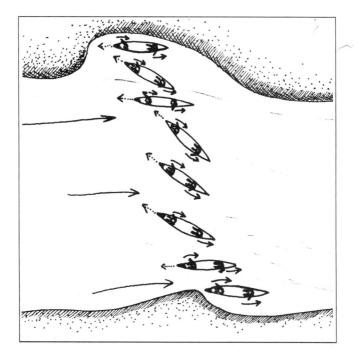

Back Ferry

Fallen trees or "sweepers" overhanging the outside bend of a river are true fast-water hazards. When approaching the bend in a river the canoeist's first reaction is to manoeuvre around the turn like a race car driver keeping to the inside of the track. The problem is that the main current of the river is heading for the outside bend of the river. This current will grab the stern of the canoe and take you broadside toward the sweeper, pinning you against the fallen tree.

When approaching a sweeper at a bend in the river you must do the unthinkable: head directly for it. When you reach the bend in the river you must "back ferry" the canoe to the inside bend of the river. With the stern of the canoe pointing upstream and tending away from the hazard, backpaddle vigorously and the current will move you across the river and away from the sweeper. To ensure enough control you should make sure that the canoe is moving considerably slower than the river current.

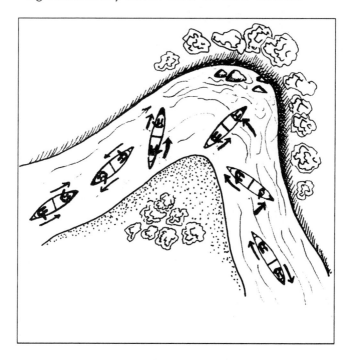

Eddying In & Eddying Out

Behind every major rock or sharp bend in the river there will be a place where the current suddenly changes direction and creates something called an "eddy." Canoeists use these calm sections of the river as an escape hatch from what's down river. The eddy can provide a place to pull in and consider the next move.

Getting your canoe into an eddy, however, is not an easy task and it's quite easy to miss the eddy altogether and find yourself heading downstream, either backwards or broadside to the current.

To enter an eddy (paddling tandem) position the canoe directly along the "eddy line" (a visible line in the water where the main current rushes around the obstacle on one side and the calm waters of the eddy begin on the other). Now, with a strong out-stretched draw from the bow on the side of the eddy and a sweep from the stern on the opposite side, turn the canoe into the calm waters of the eddy.

To exit the eddy drive the canoe out into the current with a combined draw and high brace (leaning out downstream) at the bow and a sweep at the stern. The bow paddler maintains the brace right up until the canoe has pivoted around and is facing downstream. Do not hesitate during this manoeuvre or you'll find yourself swimming down the rest of the run. Peeling out of an eddy requires more skill and balance than peeling in. Before attempting either you should first practice on open water or on a small slow-moving stream.

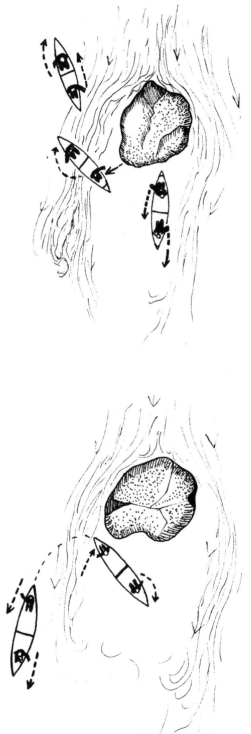

THE ART OF LINING

Picture yourself getting out of your canoe at the foot of the rapids to search out the portage only to find the beginning of a very long out-of-the-way path making its way up a steep mound of rock. The rapids ahead are cluttered with sharp pieces of granite, making a safe run impossible. It quickly becomes obvious that the best option is to slowly maneuver your canoe downstream by walking along the dry shoreline with your boat and cargo floating down on a leash. You proceed to unsnarl your entanglement of nylon rope and attempt a technique called "lining."

Lining a canoe down powerful rapids is not as simple as some people make it out to be. It took countless out-of-the-way portages before I finally built up my skill level to successfully attempt this seasoned art form. The following is the "text-book" elucidation — keep in mind that practice makes perfect!

Lining with two ropes takes a little more rehearsing than with one rope attached to the stern. This advanced technique, however, gives you much more control of the canoe as it races downstream. To attach your two lengths of rope (27 yards/25 meters long and 1/4 inch/6mm thick) I find Bill Mason's bridle knot to be the most effective: take a length of your tracking line and double back one end of the rope approximately two yards (two meters). Then knot both ends together in the center. Now place the two short ends of rope under the bow, so the knot is positioned under the canoe, right on the centerline, and tie the ends to the outer portions of the canoe seat. Repeat the same procedure with the other length of tracking line at the stern. With the main length of rope positioned directly under the canoe you place the point of pull on the centerline; this prevents the canoe from tipping when you're pulling it across a current.

It is up to you to track the canoe downstream alone, adjusting both ropes, or with a companion, one holding the bow rope and the other the stern. I find lining in pairs requires complete communication and coordination. After seeing the arguments thtat can erupt when canoe partners attempt to line together, I always line solo.

Lining alone you must adjust the comparative lengths of the two ropes and regulate the angle of the canoe relative to the current. The force of the water will push against the canoe, skirting it back and forth and allowing you to place it in the desired position.

Having the stern pointed upstream and the packs weighing down the bow gives you more maneuverability and lessens the chance of the canoe digging into the water and swamping. Also try to avoid eddies where the canoe is forced upstream with the current; itmay swing broadside when forced back into the mainstream. Remember that lining is an art form, a technique where finesse beats out brute strength.

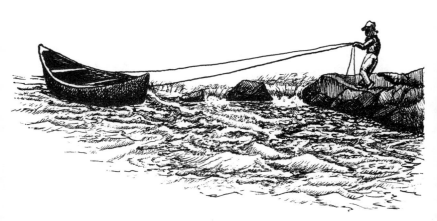

Chapter Twelve:

Darkness & Solitude

LOOKING AT THE ADVANTAGES OF
TRAVELING AT NIGHT

Years ago, while attending college in Sault Ste. Marie, I befriended a classmate, an Ojibway native named Jim Black. Jim and I spent many weekends together in the bush, especially during the winter months.

During one weekend in January, Jim and I decided to travel throughout the night. The temperature had dropped so much that we kept from freezing by staying on the move.

Ever since that bitter, cold night in the Sault I've traveled in darkness, not necessarily due to dropping temperatures, but rather because of the mood that being in the bush at night generates. It gives you an unforgettable feeling of worth.

Paddling at night has to be one of the best ways to experience darkness, with only a skin of cloud blanketing the moon's light. Traveling solo I find myself windbound for days on end. Instead of praying that the next day will bring calm waters, I break camp at midnight, taking advantage of the peaceful night air.

Once I found myself canoeing Georgian Bay's North Channel in almost complete darkness. The night was filled with sights and sounds. Drifting through blackness, with only the odd haze of northern lights to brighten up the sky, I followed the shoreline by listening to the water sucking and gurgling under the bank.

Around 2:00 a.m. I stopped paddling and coasted, letting the cool evening air descend on me. My sixth sense suddenly caused me to turn around and I came eye to eye with a timber wolf watching me from the shore. I considered halting my extended solo trip along the channel right then and there. I had to question my sanity and my safety — alone on Georgian Bay, surrounded by an unknown landscape, not another human for miles. I thrust my wooden blade into the black water and hastily made my escape.

A few minutes later, the light of the moon, un-draped by a band of clouds, illuminated the dark figure of the lone wolf standing on a rocky ledge. The wolf was following me along the shore. Embar-rassed by my previous cowardly actions, I did the unthinkable. I paddled toward the shore and gave a loud yelp. The wolf howled back, then another and another. I was moved by the wolves' singing and spent the rest of the night drifting through the dark-ness never once feeling afraid or alone.

GOING ALONE

How Solitude Can Reveal the Meaning of Life

Canada's guru of canoeing, the late Bill Mason, once remarked about solo tripping, "All of my life people have been telling me you should never travel alone. But it's interesting; I've never been told that by anybody who's ever done it." After all I have read and written on the benefits of venturing solo, Mason's simplicity says it best.

Many cultures have used solitude as a type of initiation into the meaning of life. Natives regarded aloneness as a way for shamans to conjure up magic. The Ojibway looked at wilderness solitude with reverence, a place for them to discover their own individual identity as well as to build character. After fasting alone, they believed a vision would grant each brave his guardian angel.

My Ojibway friend, Jim Black, told me of his vision quest. To him it was a time for regeneration, a cleansing of the body and mind, and the realization of nature's powerful magic.

My first solo trip was years ago along the Root River, north of Sault Ste. Marie. I battled loneliness for the first few days, spending each night curled up in the fetal position, wide awake and jumping at the night sounds. But every time I felt spooked, I reminded myself how many others had traveled alone before me and gained insight from solitude. That realization marked a turning point in my emotions. Complete loneliness was suddenly transformed into a sense of freedom, an invigorating and exciting awareness of the life around as well as within me. It didn't take long before every little noise that had kept me awake was soon lulling me to sleep.

Apart from the insightful aspects of solo travel there are many other positive points: you can make camp where and when you want, prepare food pleasing to your taste buds, travel when you think it is necessary, and relax when you believe it to be appropriate.

After an extended solo adventure I think back to my fears. Amazingly enough, what unsettles me most is not the loneliness which at times creeps up, the moment when complete darkness blankets the campsite, or being challenged by foul weather. It is when the trip is over and I am driving away from my place of vision and have to prepare myself mentally for the jam-packed expressway, crowded with thousands of people. More than once I have turned tail on one of the cut-offs, phoned home to let someone know of my altered plans, and then headed back out into the wilds for a few extra days — alone and content.

Chaper Thirteen:

Camp Critters

One of the best forms of entertainment staged in the northern woods for any camper are the crazy antics played out by the everyday camp critter. Performances range from stand-up comedy — an inquisitive chipmunk stealing tidbits of trailmix — to suspenseful drama when a bothersome bear wanders through camp. Of course the outdoor theatrical performance wouldn't be complete without wonderful musical interludes with the orchestra made up of the loon as the soprano, an assortment of baritone wolves, and a great-horned owl who keeps the back-beat rhythm.

Here's a profile of some of the actors you'll probably see taking part in a guaranteed sold-out show at the Wilderness Theater — don't miss the next performance!

The Loon

The moment you hear the primeval call of the loon, one of the earth's oldest birds, echoing across the lake you know you're in the wilderness. Its series of wails, yodels, and haunting laughter are a symbol of the north country, a sound hat lulls you to sleep at night while you lie snug in your sleeping bag and wakes you up early enough to witness the morning mist before the sun burns it off the lake.

These various calls mean a great number of things: an expression of alarm, a statement of territorial rights, and even a simple hello. The distinctive yodel that is usually heard at night comes from separate males talking to one another from lake to lake. Each bird has its own distinct yodel, so listen carefully. If it wants to show aggression, the male loon stands up on the water with its feet flapping wildly, like a tap dancer on a hard wooden floor.

You can find the common loon where lakes are deep enough to dive for fish and to escape predators, as well as providing a long-enough runway for it to run across the water's surface and take flight.

Unlike most other water birds which have air-filled bones, the loon has a solid bone structure.

The extra weight makes it difficult for the bird to take to the air but allows it to sink rapidly beneath the surface to depths of 200 feet (60 meters) or more. These great divers can baffle even the most sharp-eyed canoeist. Many times you'll find yourself waiting patiently for the loon to resurface, wondering where on earth the bird has gone. The fact is that the crafty bird has actually slipped up several times for a quick breath of air and sunk back down before you could spot it again.

With its added weight and webbed toes acting like a frogman's flippers, the loon is well adapted to an aquatic lifestyle. If only the bird could be as graceful on land! The loon's legs are so far back on its body that the bird has a hard enough time standing, let alone running, on solid ground. If chased on land it must quickly head for the safety of the water by pushing itself along on its belly, scrambling with its wings and toes.

Keep an eye out for a decline in loon populations on the lakes you visit on a regular basis. Wave action from motor boats constantly disturb their nests and the effects of toxic pollutants in the water or acid rain are starving them out.

If you spot a loon sitting quietly on her nest, do not approach for a photo. Once you vex the bird she will most likely abandon her nest completely.

Common Merganser

This diving duck is usually spotted swimming close to shore with its half-dozen or more goslings waddling close behind. The female has a distinctive, bright, chestnut-coloured head and crest, while the male has a white breast, a dark glossy head, and lacks the female's crest. Don't mistake the common merganser with the more northern red-breasted merganser. The male red-breasted has a crest and a streaked breast. The female's crest is dull in colour and has a full, pale, white-coloured collar and breast.

The merganser has been given the nickname "sawbill" for its long orange serrated bill used for snatching fish while swimming underwater, but it's more noted by canoeists for its amazing ability to float care-free down a raging rapid and come out at the end without a scratch. If you want to know the safest route down through whitewater, follow the bird's path.

Don't look for their nests on the ground; the common merganser is like the wood duck and nests in the hollows of dead trees. Ducks nesting in trees! What will Mother Nature come up with next?

Great-blue Heron

During a spring outing in late May you might be lucky enough to spot a heron rookery, busy with a congregation of great blue herons sitting quietly in their elaborate stick structures swaying in the wind or homing in with their wings outstretched to almost six feet (two meters). Spring is the only time male and female great blue herons gather together. They spend most of the year as loners, searching the shallows of a lake, pond or river for fish and frogs. They can stand frozen in the water for hours waiting for their prey to come to them. Then with amazing accuracy they lash out with their long, sharp bills spearing the unsuspecting dinner and swallowing it whole. The big bird's defensive strategy while in its nest is to "whitewash" or vomit on any predator that attempts to climb up. In close quarters the heron will jab its javelin-like bill directly at its enemy's eyes.

In flight the great blue heron will usually squawk or croak. Look for the long skinny legs dragging behind the tail and the dropped neck. I've found they prefer to fly at night: sometimes when you are sitting around the the evening fire, "big bird" suddenly comes out of the darkness for a surprise landing right beside your camp.

Gray Jay

I swear that gray jays, fluffy grey-feathered birds with white forehead and collar, come equipped with some type of homing device locked on to soft-hearted camp cooks. These birds are legendary for their bold but friendly approach to camps, panhandling any scrap of food they can quickly snatch up in their stubby bills. They have a preference for greasy bacon, baked beans, and my special bannock covered in syrup.

There are as many stage names for this bird of the boreal forest as there are favorite snacks. Some ornithologists still call it the "Canada Jay." Loggers nicknamed it "camp robber," a fitting moniker. And people living in the north prefer to call it the "whiskeyjack." It is not known if the bird has a taste for liquor, but the name was derived most likely from the Algonkian word Wisakedjak used to describe the Trickster — a supernatural shape-shifting spirit that loved to play pranks on people camped in the forest.

Chipmunk

The natives tell of a time when it was undecided if the earth would be covered in complete darkness or continously bask in sunlight. It was up to two of the forest animals to decide: the bear fought for night and the chipmunk opted for day.

Most of the animals placed their bet on the bear, thinking the bruin's strength and size would overpower the tiny chipmunk. But when the fight began, the quick and agile rodent easily outmaneuvered the bear. After a long fight the bear finally caught the chipmunk under its big paw and it looked as if darkness would soon cover the earth forever. But suddenly the spry chipmunk squeezed its slender body out from under the bruin's grasp and was free.

The battle thus ended in a tie, allowing the earth to have both night and day, and to this day the chipmunk bears the scars across its back to remind everyone of the fight between darkness and light.

Today the chipmunk's mystic war wounds (five dark brown or black stripes down its back) help camouflage it from aerial predators, as the stripes blend in with the dark shadows of twigs and plants.

Chipmunks spend a lot of their time underground. They construct a system of burrows twisting and turning three feet (a meter) beneath the surface and equipped with storage tunnels and escape hatches. It is almost impossible to locate the main entrance of the tunnel. The chipmunk makes an extra effort to rid the area of any trace of its presence by storing the excavated dirt in a work hole and then removing it later by stuffing it in its cheek pouches and spreading it evenly across the forest floor.

If you spot a chipmunk chasing another through your campsite, with its tail jerking and making loud chirping noises, it is probably because the one being chased has just robbed the other of its prized food cache. Chipmunks are solitary creatures and only pair up during mating season. They devote most of their time to gathering and storing food underground. The chipmunk does not hibernate but simply reduces its metabolism during the cold winter months. It will awaken periodically in the winter to munch on its food supplies, or, if the weather is mild enough, it will even exit from its tunnel and forage above ground.

Red Squirrel

Have you ever found yourself snug in your sleeping bag listening to the calm of morning only to be interrupted by a bombardment of pine cones falling on the roof of your tent? And when you unzip the front door, poking your head out to make sure the sky isn't falling, you hear the noisy chatter of a red squirrel as he gets a bull's eye on your noggin with a resin-covered pine cone?

Being bombarded by clipped seed canisters is no way to greet the morning, but it's a fair price to pay to witness the antics of one of the most delightful camp critters in the northern woods. No matter where you go you'll spot the red squirrel busy gathering food above in the canopy of a coniferous stand or hear it chattering loudly from the branches, scolding trespassers invading its territory.

The cones the red squirrel clips from the trees are gathered in huge piles to dine on at a later date. The food cache is usually in a shady area or inside hollow logs to stop the cones from drying up and dispersing their seeds. The red squirrel is the most carnivorous squirrel in the forest, adding to its diet mice, insects, bird eggs, and fledglings. It gathers mushrooms and hangs them on branches to dry before storing them. In fact, their hyperactivity, from constantly flicking their tail to scrambling up a tree trunk at 15 miles an hour (25 km/h), is due to their high-energy diet.

Porcupine

One early spring I was camped on a northern lake under a full moon. Everything seemed peaceful until I was surprised by a loud, eerie cry from outside the tent. The sound ranged from a baby's whimper to the wail of a banshee. It scared me silly, to be quite honest, and I spent the night wrapped in my sleeping bag, praying that morning would soon come.

In the safety of daylight I left the tent and, investigating the whereabouts of the strange noise that had haunted me throughout the night, I discovered my paddle shaft chewed to pieces. It was obvious a porcupine had visited my camp that evening and dined on my paddle, attracted by the salty sweat collected on its wooden shaft. The porcupine's passion for any piece of wood with salt on it was old news to me, but that was the first time I had ever heard the male porcupine's bizarre mating call.

I left camp in search of the loudmouth bachelor high up in a pine tree, changing his diet from paddles to pine bark. He sat content in the crook of the tree not bothered by my presence. I kept my distance from him just the same.

Contrary to popular belief, the porcupine does not shoot its 30,000 quills when approached. If you do approach it closely enough, however, it will raise the quills up on its back and attempt to swat you with its quill-infested tail. The quill is more deadly than a simple pin prick; it is tipped with hundreds of tiny barbs which help work the quill deeper and deeper into your skin the more your muscles contract. Dogs and any other animals who come face to tail with a porcupine have been known to die when a single quill works its way through the victim's brain, slowly driving it mad.

Moose

If you thought bears were the most dangerous creatures in the wilds, you're wrong. A bull moose during rutting season is more apt to tree you than a
bear. I was once awakened in the middle of the
night, horrified to discover a confused bull moose
trying to step over my tent rope. I should never have
set up camp in the middle of a portage, I guess,
but it was late and I simply couldn't go any further.

If you allow a safe distance between you and the
moose, however, photographing North America's
largest land mammal is an exhilarating experience,
to say the least.

The moose spends most of its time searching out
salt. It craves the spice so much it will wander alongside busy highways in the spring to lick the left-over
road salt off the pavement or even dive down as far
as fifteen feet (five meters) below a swamp or marsh
to eat the salty aquatic plants growing on the bottom.

The bull moose needs lots of salt to help grow
its antlers before the fall rut. After mating season,
the horns fall off, but the moose's size and craving
for salt still make it a hazard for those who get in
its way.

Chapter Foureen:

Name That Tree

White Pine

These ancient monarchs of the forest once towered more than ten storeys high, dominating the country. Then Napoleon's forces cut off the British from their major lumber source in northern Europe, forcing the British to travel to Canada for lumber. The eastern white pine, being so tall and straight, was perfect for making masts for the naval fleet and so it was the first to go.Few virgin stands are left. Only patches of the ancient pine dot the northern landscape; single mature trees rooted alongside rocky windswept shorelines remind us of the treasures the forest once held. Young pine can still be found growing back from the land that was once harvested.

The bark of a young white pine is smooth greygreen. With age, it turns rough, deeply furrowed with broad scaly edges, and grey-brown in color.The needles are soft to the touch and grow in bundles of five (remember the word "white" has five letters). The feathery silhouette of the white pine is its most distinctive characteristic, its upper portion sculptured by prevailing wind.

Red Pine

The red pine, a much hardier tree than the white, takes root in rocky outcrops and nutrient-deficient sandy soil. It is protected from extreme heat, cold, and bug infestations by its thick resin.

The bark has a reddish - or pinkish - brown tinge and becomes furrowed into long, scaly, flat ridges as it grows older.

Unlike that of the soft white pine needles growing in clusters of five, the red pine has sharply pointed needles in clusters of two.

The silhouette has an oval appearance, forming at the crown. When it grows in the open, branches cover most of its trunk.

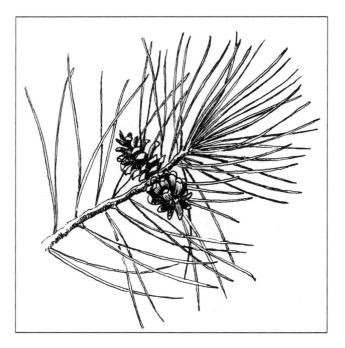

Jack Pine

The twisted, knot-ridden jack pine was bad news for the early settlers due to its ability to grow on the poorest soil.

Of all the conifer species the jack pine is the most likely to sprout first after a fire since its tightly sealed cones usually open up only when the temperature reaches 116°F (47°C).

The bark of the jack pine is reddish-brown to grey and changes to a darker brown or grey. It is flaky, and furrowed into irregular thick plates on older trees.

The needles, growing in clusters of two, are a lighter green and somewhat shorter than that of the red and white pine, and they come to a sharp point.

It is the jack pine's closed cones, however, that clearly identify this species from all the others. The cone looks similar to a piece of dried-up scat hanging on a branch.

Black and White Spruce

The black and white spruce are from the single-needle conifer group. The sharp stunted needles are attached completely around the twig, in the shape of a cigar.

One of the main differences between white and black spruce is the tip of the bud. If the bud-scale is shorter than the bud, then the tree is a white spruce. If the bud-scale grows past the tip of the bud, then it is a black spruce.

There is a difference between the silhouette of the two spruces as well. The white spruce's form is more cone-shaped, with its branches evenly concealing the trunk. The black spruce has very few branches along most of its length, except at the crown where they are bunched together.

The easiest way to tell the white and black spruce apart, however, is to look at the surrounding habitat. If your feet are wet, then the tree is a black spruce which roots in sphagnum bogs. On the other hand, the white spruce prefers well-drained, silty soils.

White Cedar

For centuries, the cedar was worshipped as the giver of life. It is also highly regarded by the average camper, not for holding spiritual life-giving powers, but for having the magical ability to get a campfire going in the midst of a downpour.

Cedar can be found in both wetland swamps and rocky outcrops due to its ability to be both rot and drought resistant. The bark is colored a light grey to reddish-brown and its needles are unlike those of any other conifers, with light green to yellow, flat, scale-like leaves.

Hemlock

The hemlock tree may be easily confused with a spruce. However, its needles are not attached completely around the twig but are flat, and lacking the cigar-shaped twig of the black and white spruce. Another difference is that the hemlock's needle has two distinct white lines on its underside.

The bark of young hemlock is scaly and orange-brown, becoming deeply furrowed and purplish grey-brown with age.

As the hemlock's trunk is filled with knots, lumberjacks hate cutting it for wood. Campers distrust the seering sparks it lets loose when burned in the campfire. Plants are unable to root in the acidic soil created by its decomposed needles. But deer couldn't survive the winter without it: they gather under the conifer's dense canopy and nibble on its low-lying branches.

Balsam Fir

Similar to the hemlock, the balsam fir needles are flat and not rounded like a spruce. They also have white lines on the underside, but usually more than two. The bark of the balsam fir, especially when young, is its most distinguishing feature. The grey, smooth skin is pocked with horizontal specks and blisters filled with resin. When you puncture the resin blister with your thumbnail, sticky sap will ooze out.

This sap is the reason most conifers, except the tamarack which loses its needles in the fall, hold their needles year-round — hence the name "evergreen." Deciduous trees must store their sap in their root system so the sugar and water mixture (mostly water) will not freeze and expand inside the branches. Without the sap the leaves die and fall to the ground every autumn. The sugar-rich sap of the evergreen, however, acts as an antifreeze and allows the conifer to hang on to its needles throughout the cold dormant season.

Chapter Fifteen:

Reading the Stars

A GUIDE TO THE BIG PICTURE IN THE SKY 182

A Guide to the Big Picture in the Sky

Have you ever paddled under a clear night sky or walked out on to a frozen lake, laid down on your back, and looked up at the stars? There's no other word to describe what you see except, "Wow!"

Star watching is at its best in the wilds, away from the reflection of city lights are. With shooting stars, blinking satellites, aircraft lights, glare from the moon, and the odd UFO, it's quite difficult at times to look up and point out a particular constellation, especially when the group of stars resembles nothing like the name given to them. It's important to note, however, that the titles of each constellation came from the wild imagination of ancient storytellers when books were yet to be written. In a way, the starlit sky is simply one big picture book relating the stories of old.

The easiest group of stars to look for are the ones which appear to be circling closest to Polaris (the North Star). The North Star sits over the North Pole and acts as the northern axis; the further a constellation is from Polaris, the more difficult it will be to keep track of it as it changes its position in the sky throughout the year.

To find the North Star ue your compass, keeping in mind that your compass needle will point to magnetic north and not true north where Polaris sits. Or you can locate it by using the Big Dipper. Once you spot the seven bright stars, four in the shape of the bowl and three as the ladle, draw an imaginary line between the two stars at the end of the bowl. Now, from the tip of the bowl follow that line three to five times its length to reach Polaris.

The Big Dipper is actually the rump and tail of Ursa Major or the Great Bear. Many stories are told about this constellation. Natives of North America saw the ladle of the Big Dipper not as a bear's tail, but as hunters with dogs chasing the bear in circles around the northern heavens. Some tribes even connected the leaves changing color in the fall with the bear being wounded by the hunters and dripping its blood from the sky on to the trees.

Another common tale is from Greek mythology; the constellation is said to be Callisto, a paramour of Zeus. It is said that Callisto swore a vow of chasity when she became a favorite hunting partner of Artemis, goddess of hunting. But one afternoon, while she was resting under a tree, Zeus caught a glimpse of her and was entranced by her beauty. He changed into the form of Artemis and approached Callisto. When she reached out to embrace her friend, Zeus showed his true form and had his way with her.

Zeus returned to Olympus and left poor Callisto pregnant. She later gave birth to a son, Arcas. Eventually Hera, the wife of Zeus, found out that her husband had been unfaithful to her and took revenge on Callisto by transforming her into a bear, now making the hunter the hunted.

Callisto supposedly wandered through the woods for years, until one day she met up with her son, Arcas. When she went to him, however, he did not recognize his mother in her animal form. He would have speared Callisto if Zeus had not intervened by changing Arcas into the same form as his mother. He grabbed them both by the tail and hurled them into heaven; in doing so, he stretched out their tails.

When Hera found out that Zeus had saved Callisto, she once again showed her rage by demanding Tethys and Oceanus, gods of the sea and Hera's foster parents, never to allow the Great Bear to bathe. And to this day poor Callisto has yet to set below the horizon into the waters of the northern hemisphere.

NORTH SKY

MAY 1 : 12:00 P.M.
MAY 15: 11:00 P.M.
JUNE 1: 10:00 P.M.
JUNE 15: 9:00 P.M.
JULY 1: 8:00 P.M.

The Little Dipper

Ursa Minor or the Little Bear is more commonly known as the Little Dipper. If you have properly located the North Star you will quickly realize that it is the last star on the Little Dipper's ladle. Often this constellation was thought to be the most important because it contained Polaris. The Arabs called it "the Guiding One." The Chinese named it Tou Mu, a goddess who saved shipwrecked sailors with her supernatural powers and was later transported up into the sky. Ancient Norsemen labelled it the "Hill of Heaven," home of the guardian of the rainbow bridge joining heaven and earth. Native North Americans believed it to be a young girl who appeared to a group of lost braves and showed them the way home by pointing up at Polaris. And returning to Greek mythology and the story of Callisto, the Little Bear is Arcas, the Big Bear's son.

Bootes — Guardian Of The Bear

Despite what you may have been told, the North Star is not the brightest star in the sky. During the summer the star Arcturus, part of the Bootes constellation, burns 120 times more radiant and is 24 times larger than our sun.

To find Arcturus and the Bootes constellation, follow the curve of the Big Dipper's ladle to the next brightest star. The group of stars, including Arcturus, is in the shape of a kite or ice-cream cone and is thought to be the guardian of the Big Bear, guiding it around Polaris.

Draco — The Dragon

The group of stars spread out between the Big Dipper and Little Dipper and beyond, is the constellation Draco, the dragon. The tip of the dragon's tail is closely in line between the the tip of the Big Dipper's ladle and Polaris (the tip of the Little Dipper's ladle). The twisting body snakes around the Little

185

Dipper's bowl and then points away, ending in a rectangle of four stars which form the dragon's head.

Greek legend tells that the Hesperides, daughters of Atlas, guarded the precious tree on which grew golden apples, given to Hera as a wedding present by her husband Zeus. The daughters turned out to be untrustworthy, however, by picking the apples. So Hera replaced them with a giant dragon. Hercules, the great hero, was slain by the dragon with poisoned arrows when he tried to steal some apples. Hera placed the dragon in the sky for its loyalty, and called the constellation Draco.

I've just touched on a few star tales; already the night sky sounds like a regular soap opera. To search out more constellations you need to pack along a good star map or chart along with pocket guides to the stars such as Peterson's *Field Guide to the Stars* and *Planets or The Backyard Astronomer's Guide.* Hold the star chart up to the night sky with one hand, your field guide in the other, and with your flashlight sticking out of your mouth lie back, relax, and let the stars tell you a tale.

Chapter Sixteen:

Snap-shot Memories

HOW TO BE AN ARTIST WITH A CAMERA

How to be an Artist with a Camera

Killarney Provincial Park is a magnet for artists, especially during the fall when hoards of people visit the park to capture the autumn colors on canvas. Being an avid photographer I also love spending time in the park when the leaves are changing. But at times I feel as if my camera is not welcome alongside the artists and their palettes. One particular trip I stood beside a painter and took a snap-shot of the landscape he was attempting to put on canvas. "It's much quicker to capture it on film than on canvas," I joked. The man quickly responded, "It may be quicker, but you can't call it art!"

The artist was right in thinking a photo print could not compare to a painting; his brush has more power to capture a particular mood than any camera lens. But I strongly disagree that photography is not an art and that the mechanics of a camera cannot capture memories just as effectively as a painter with his brush.

To capture my memories of time spent in the wilds I use a 35 mm camera, equipped with a regular 50 mm, a wide angle and 80-200 zoom lens. Any other lenses carried along are for pleasure, not necessity. Don't get hooked into purchasing and packing a pile of equipment you will probably never use. When I first started out, I spent a small fortune on equipment which was stolen from my campsite while I was visiting the outhouse. It was the best thing that ever happened to me. I couldn't afford to buy anything except the essentials, which I still use today.

A good tripod is a must, to compensate for an unsteady hand. I also bring along extra batteries, a skylight filter to protect the lens from being scratched, and a release shutter for those long exposures of the evening sky.

A variety of waterproof bags can be used to store your gear if you're canoeing or hiking through a rainstorm. These can range from ammunition boxes purchased at the army surplus to an expensive Pelican case. I use a River Runner bag which can be filled with air, keeping the camera above water during an upset and protecting it from knocks and bumps. It has some disadvantages: I have a hard time pulling everything out when that perfect picture runs right past me, and, if left inside on a damp and cold morning, the lenses tend to fog up.

Film is really important. Slide film is best, even if you don't own a slide projector. Kodachrome and Fujichrome (Velvia) are top quality.

Bringing along an expensive camera is not a necessity, however. I take photographs for a living, but people I camp with are happy with a good compact camera. In fact, some have taken better shots with their auto focus, auto exposure, and auto flash pocket cameras. But the compact cameras do not have an assortment of lenses and on some models you cannot override the auto exposure and you lose your creative control. The sharpness of the lenses cannot be compared with those of a professional photographer's camera.

Chapter Seventeen:

A Campfire Tale

THE PURPLE GORILLA

I've never really felt comfortable telling ghost stories to a group of young campers around a campfire. The problem is, when the moment comes to douse the flames and call it a night, the terrified kids curl up in their canvas tents, then stay awake jumping at their own shadows.

On the other hand, it is also very difficult to disappoint a group of enthusiastic youngsters who have been brainwashed through their early years into thinking that spooky stories belong to any true outdoor adventure. So, when I'm asked to spin a tale of horror around the campfire, I make everyone happy by telling the hair-raising tale of the dreaded Purple Gorilla. It goes like this:

I had a friend once, a shy, unusual fellow named Myron.

Unlike the other kids on the block Myron never had a normal pet like a dog or cat. Instead, he kept his very own pet gorilla. Not just an everyday gorilla, however, but a huge, purple gorilla.

One night Myron asked me for a favor. He was going out of town and wanted me to take care of his purple gorilla for him.

To be honest, I was a bit hesitant at first, but Myron assured me the animal was quite tame, so I agreed. Myron handed me a list of instructions and headed out the door.

As I read through the list, noting what to feed him and such, I noticed a special note Myron had placed at the bottom. It said: "Whatever you do, don't touch the purple gorilla."

Later that night, after I had set up the gorilla's sleeping arrangements inside the iron cage Myron had left for me, I wondered why my friend did not want me to touch his pet gorilla; I mean, the creaturelooked quite innocent.

However, I obeyed his command, dished out the colorful ape's dinner, and headed upstairs for bed.

Half-way through the night, restless and sleepless, I decided I couldn't stand it any longer. I had to find out why Myron instructed me not to touch his pet gorilla. Slowly, I crept down to the basement where the creature slept contentedly behind iron bars.

Carefully I squirmed my hand through the cage and quickly touched the purple gorilla.

Suddenly, the hairy monster leaped up, bent the iron bars wide open, and bellowed a tremendous roar. I sprang backwards and raced back up the stairs.

The wild giant ape followed and chased me over such obstacles as the living-room couch and kitchen table. The intelligent beast was becoming wise to my fancy maneuvers around the household furniture, so I did what any normal person would do while being chased by a purple gorilla — I ran outside, got into my car, and hightailed it down the street.

With the pedal to the metal I made record time around the block only to find out that my escape vehicle had run out of gas.

I jumped out of the car and ran down the sidewalk, keeping an eye out for the gorilla. I built up a good lead until I stumbled on a crack in the pavement, and tripped on the hard cement.

Seconds later, I spied the creeping shadow of Myron's gorilla. Purple sweat dripped from its hairy armpits as the animal breathed his foul-smelling breath down the back of my neck. It was obvious that the jig was up!

As I lay helpless on the sidewalk, the beast slowly lowered his sharp clawstowards my exposed throat.

As my life passed before my eyes I asked myself "Why? Why didn't I listen to Myron? Why did I touch the purple gorilla in the first place?"

It was too late for regrets, for the animal's powerful paws were inches from my limp and quivering flesh.

Death seemed only a moment away. The gorilla tapped me lightly on the shoulder, sprang up, and roared, "You're it!"

Believe me, it gets them every time!

ACKNOWLEGEMENTS

Writing this book would have been impossible without the help of many people. I would first like to thank my father who taught me to take the time to appreciate a sunset, kicked me out of my sleeping bag early in the morning to listen to the wail of the loon, and introduced me to the fresh smell of coffee brewing on an open fire.

I would also like to thank my regular camp cronies, Scott Roberts, Brian Reid, Mike Walker, and Doug Galloway for helping to create so many good memories.

A special thanks goes to Dave Fewster whose artistic talents brought this book to life.

As well, special thanks to the staff at Hiker's Haven in Oakville for all their expertise, and most of all, their friendship.

And last, but certainly not least, I would like to thank my wife, Alana Hammill, for proofreading page after page of manuscript, adding her "secret" recipe to the pages, being an excellent canoe partner, and most of all, holding my hand every step of the way.